KNOW THE GAME SERIES

ORIENTEERING

by

J. D. Watson of the Scottish Orienteering Association

Contents

PART ONE—The Competitor

	Page
What is Orienteering	2
The Orienteering Event	3
Orienteering Maps	6
Orienteering Skills (Map Interpretation and Route Selection, The Compass, Measurement of Distance, Map Memory)	17
Types of Orienteering	26
Becoming a Group or School Leader	27
Training points	28

PART TWO—Competitions and Organisation

	Page
Preparing for a competition	30
Timetable for an Open Club Event	42
Safety	43
Control Terminology	43
Map Making	44
Glossary of Terms	45
Some Important Addresses	46
Age Grouping in British Orienteering (as from January, 1973)	47

Colour Maps appear in two sections:- pages 9-16 and pages 33-40.

PART 1 THE COMPETITOR

What is Orienteering?

Orienteering is a competitive sport in which those taking part navigate from point to point with the aid of special map and compass, as quickly and efficiently as possible by whatever route they interpret as best for them. It is a widely known and well established sport elsewhere in Europe (especially in Scandinavia where in July 1972 the Annual Five-Day Swedish O-Ringen event attracted almost 10,000 competitors) but the sport was only recently established in Britain — first with the foundation of the Scottish Orienteering Association in 1962, the English Orienteering Association in 1965 and the British Orienteering Federation in 1967. Today the B.O.F. adminsters orienteering through twelve regional associations.

In Britain the sport first originated in Scotland where opportunities for the many different types of orienteering are provided by the varied topographical features of the countryside. Whether on forest or mountainside the orienteer, with the aid of his map and compass, can learn to "read" the detail of the countryside as easily as if he were reading a book.

But though Scotland most closely resembles the classical orienteering country of Scandinavia, other parts of Britain have proved eminently suitable. Wherever there is a piece of accessible forest, heath, moorland or occasionally even a public park, orienteering may be practised.

Essentially orienteering requires the participants to solve a series of problems concerning the planning and execution of the quickest route over a course usually covering a few kilometres. The course is set with a series of check points between a start line and a finishing line. It requires both intelligence and stamina to cover the course in the most efficient manner, taking into account any difficulties that may be caused by steep gradients, the weather or vegetation for instance. So orienteering teaches the participant to assess, understand and "read" the countryside.

On each "leg" of a course the skilful "setter" tries to test particular orienteering skills and forces the runner to make continuous navigational decisions.

Thus this is a sport which may appeal to all ages and to both sexes. It may be adapted and varied in an almost infinite number of ways to provide an enjoyable, challenging and rewarding sport, whether organised as a team event, an individual competition or a combination of both.

Not only the Forestry Commission but also private landowners have proved only too willing to see that the vast acres of Britain's woodland and rough ground be put to responsible recreational use.

Orienteering takes place throughout the year, with virtually no closed season. The climax is in the summer, with the British Championships being held in June. Other minor and major events take place throughout the year, with each region holding its own championship and many other club or district events besides.

While many orienteers compete almost without a stop, with a hundred or so even spending a few summer weeks orienteering in Europe, others can pick and choose — either an event here and there, or perhaps orienteering for a particular season of their own choice. Many others committed to several sports, prefer to use orienteering as a close season training, either in summer or winter.

The following pages are offered as a guide to the beginner feeling his way through the first stages of the sport. However, orienteering as it has developed cannot be undertaken by the beginner alone. He must attend someone else's competition; he must "come and try it". Almost all competitions have courses designed to facilitate the beginner of whatever age. Many clubs and associations run events and days where beginners can "come and try it".

An Orienteering Event

From your regional secretary you will be able to find which events in your area are most suitable for novices. Having chosen your competition, you will probably find that it takes place on a Sunday, starting mid-morning. Start-times may spread over several hours with competitors leaving at minute intervals. Arrive in good time; you will be pretty busy in the half hour before you set off on your first orienteering course.

What shall I wear?

The serious orienteer wears a light, nylon orienteering suit and special studded shoes. (Fig. 1). Most wear long nylon trousers, but depending on undergrowth and time of year, some prefer to wear shorts, and stockings with built-in shin protection.

A beginner should wear clothes which he or she regards as sensible for tracking though the forest or across the moorland, taking into account the weather, one's age, whether one intends a run, or perhaps just a brisk walk. Above all avoid silly clothing; especially in winter, gym shoes, shorts and a running vest are not enough. Many boys and girls begin more sensibly with jeans, an anorak and hockey or soccer boots.

Douglas Murray, 1971–2 British Junior Champion wearing normal orienteer gear.
Fig. 1a. Nylon Suit with pockets for control card, description etc.
Fig. 1b. Studded orienteering shoes.

Fig. 1a.   Fig. 1b.

There are several different kinds of orienteering, but your first competition will most likely be "Cross Country Orienteering" where controls set out in the forest must be visited in a certain sequence.

Car parking is usually provided by the event organisers. Remember that most competitions may be inaccessible to public transport — though special beginners' courses may well be near a built up area.

On arrival you report to Registration (see fig. 2) which may take the form of a tent, a convenient building or perhaps a car window, depending on the sophistication of the event. Here you enter, pay your entry fee (10p or 20p is normal) receive a special orienteering map, (see page 9, fig. 8), a list of control descriptions and a competitor's card, which will contain a start time. You may also be able to hire a compass, probably a Silva compass (see page 18, fig. 17) though other less popular types are available.

Adjacent to registration there may be maps posted showing map corrections. These may be genuine corrections, e.g. showing a new forest road, or they may be pointing out areas of danger, for example high crags. Whatever the information, copy it carefully on to your map.

From now on until a few minutes before the start time the orienteer has three main tasks:

a) Prepare the map
b) Study the map
c) Get to the start and warm up.

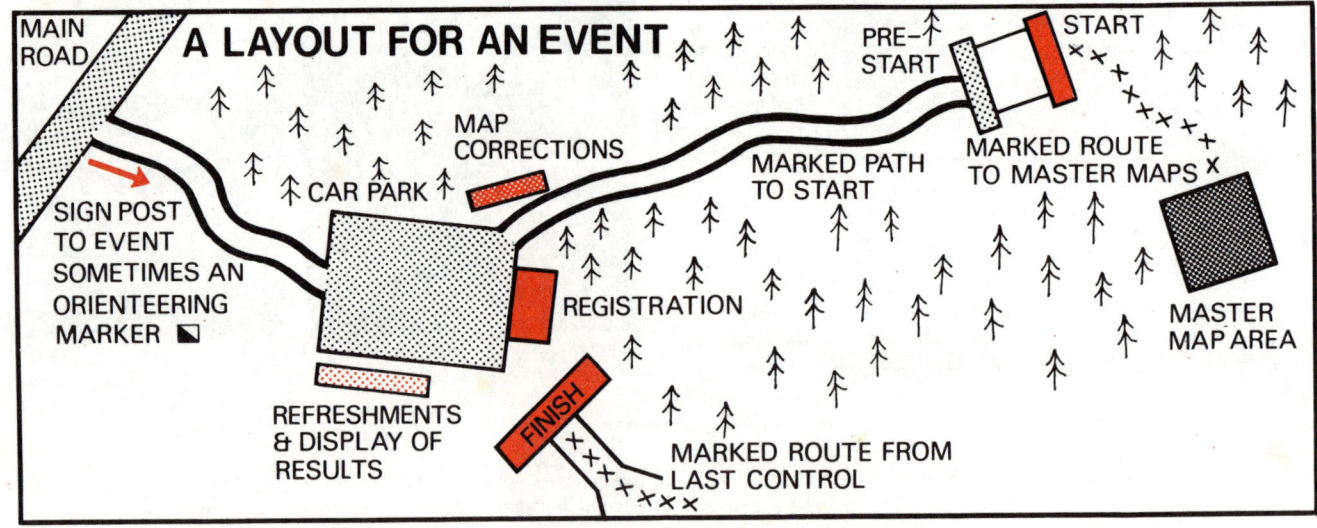

Fig. 2.

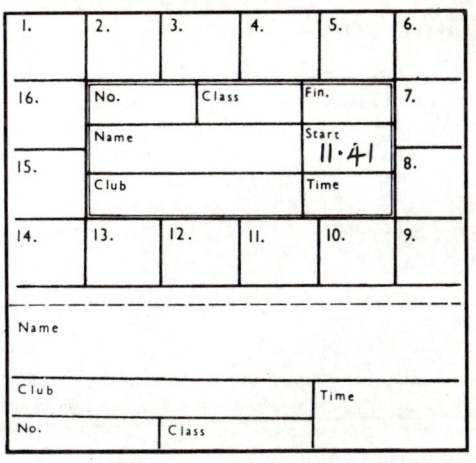

Fig. 3.
A Control Card.

c) The start may be some distance from registration. In the case of beginners this is useful, allowing time and distance for the study of the map. If you are a beginner in charge of beginners insist that those in your charge sensibly spend the walk to the start studying the map.

By the time you reach the start area you are most likely to have warmed up. But if registration is close to the start then deliberate warming up may be necessary.

The start area may be divided into Pre-Start and Start (see fig. 2). At pre-start competitors are marshalled a minute or so before their start time. Often the competitor's card contains a stub (see fig. 3) which is torn off and handed in at pre-start as proof of starting.

As the minutes proceed (usually competitors leave at minute intervals) the orienteer moves to the start. Finally the last few seconds are counted down, the starter blows his whistle . . . and you are off! For the first score or so yards — or better still metres, as orienteering has always been very metric conscious, you follow a streamer marked route to the Master Maps (see fig. 2 and page 10, fig. 9). At the master map area you quickly find the map for your course. Usually an official will be on hand to guide you.

a) The beginner's map will require little of the sometimes involved doctoring of the champion's — who will often cut his map down to the smallest possible size, covering it with a transparent, adhesive, waterproof, plastic film. A novice's map is best placed whole in a waterproof map case or polythene bag.

b) Study the map. Find out where you are. By the time you get to a competition you will know the special orienteering symbols shown in the legend. You will also have learnt how to orientate your map. As you move off ensure that you are tied to the map every step of the way. Know exactly where you are all the time. Check the surveyor's interpretation of particular features. What does *he* mean by a "forest road", a "footpath", or by "dense vegetation".

Beginners Course	Control letter
1 THE STREAM & PATH JUNCTION	B
2 THE TOWER	H
3 THE WELL	M
4 THE CLEARING, SOUTH END	Z

Fig. 4. *Control Descriptions.*

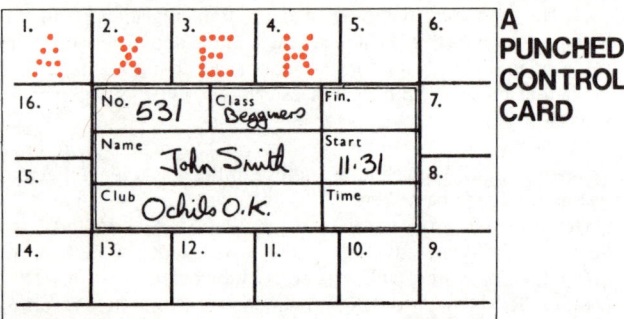

Fig. 5.

Carefully copy the various controls onto your own map. Remember to join up the controls with lines and include the control numbers. For this purpose a red ball-point pen is probably the most useful writing tool; though those covering their maps with adhesive film may well use Chinagraph pencils. Put your map in your map case and you are on your own.

You must now orienteer from control to control in the correct sequence until you reach the finish (see fig. 2 and page 31, fig. 24). Each control will be located exactly at the point shown on the map and will be in the form of a red and white banner (fig. 5) displaying the control letter shown on your description sheet. Fixed to it or hanging adjacent to it will be a punch (fig. 5) with which one punches one's competitor's card in the appropriate square.

Orienteering Maps

The map is the orienteer's most vital piece of equipment. The area used in a single orienteering event is only a few square miles in extent and the orienteer needs as much detail as possible, so maps of a fairly large scale are used. The most common scale is approximately three inches to one mile or "1:20,000" (1" on the map respresents 20,000 inches or approximately three miles on the ground). Other commonly used scales are $2\frac{1}{2}$" to one mile (1:25,000) and 6" to one mile (1:10,560).

Unfortunately it has been found that the popular Ordnance Survey 1" to one mile map simply does not show enough detail to be useful in competitive orienteering.

Originally British orienteers used the Ordnance Survey $2\frac{1}{2}$" maps and occasionally 6" maps. Permission was obtained to reproduce them in black and white through one or other of the copying processes. However, as early orienteers will never forget, such a system was far from ideal. Often poor copying obscured detail; the advantages of colour were lost and though Ordnance Survey maps may be accurate and up-to-date in urban areas this is hardly ever so in the forest.

Also orienteers frequently required information about the navigability of a piece of terrain which the Ordnance Survey was not interested in showing. Such things might include the density of the forest, areas of recent felling or windblown timber or whether the boundary is a four-foot dry stone wall or an eight-foot deer fence topped with barbed wire.

And so, in 1968 British orienteers began to produce their own maps, usually based on the Ordnance Survey 6" map, but modified and up-dated through scores of hours surveying in the

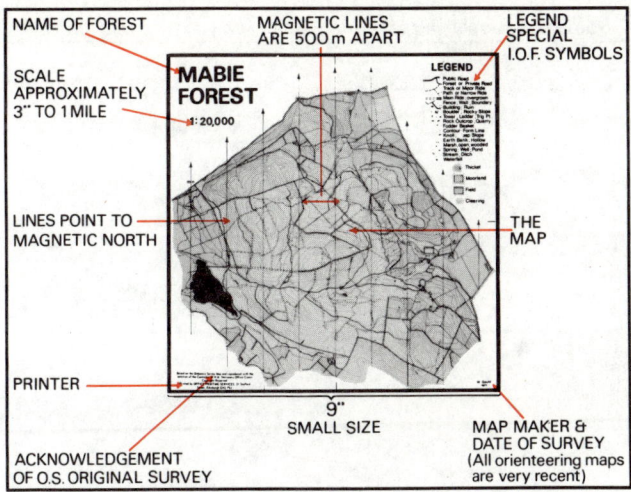

Fig. 6. *The features of a modern orienteering map.*

field and usually through the use of aerial photographs. Finally, an orienteering map is drawn according to International Orienteering Federation symbols (see page 11, fig. 10) — often with a few British variations thrown in — and is printed by one of a handful of printers recommended by the B.O.F., usually in three, four or five colours. Each map costs only a few pence.

The maps differ from those you are used to in the following respects:

(a) The Size — The maps are small, certainly no more than 12" long and are specifically of the area being used for the event. They usually go into your map case without folding.

(b) There is no grid — unlike on Ordnance Survey maps, and hence no sheet number. Maps are usually named, e.g. Ranmore Common, Torrie Forest, Mabie Forest.

(c) The North-South lines — These are lines pointing to Magnetic North and are drawn 500 metres apart. On almost all other maps such lines would point to True North (the direction of the North Pole) or to a slightly arbitrary direction such as Grid North (which varies slightly from True North on O.S. maps). Having magnetic lines is a great advantage as we shall see when discussing the use of the compass. Some may argue that magnetic north changes, as indeed it does, but a change of $\frac{1}{2}°$ every 8 years makes this of little significance.

(d) The scale of the map — This will probably be 1:20,000 (approximately 3" to one mile) which will be strange to you. However, apart from producing maps of a very convenient size, allowing just the right amount of detail, it is also very easy to use. One edge of your compass is graduated in millimetres (see page 18, fig. 17). At a scale of 1:20,000, one millimetre represents 20 metres, five millimetres represent 100 metres.

(e) The production — The map may be based on the O.S. map or it may be an entirely original "photogrametrically" based map. Orienteers are now beginning to produce maps absolutely from scratch.

(f) The date — The map is likely to be very recent. For important competitions, from national championships down to club races, entirely new maps may be surveyed and printed for each event.

(g) The legend — Finally and most obviously the symbols (called the legend) are different from the conventional ones on O.S. maps. The reason for their differing from the conventional signs is because the maps can then conform to an international code bearing the same legend as those in other orienteering countries. Also orienteering symbols are designed to show the information which is significant for purposes of navigation on foot. New orienteering maps are also very clear and easy to read — an extremely important point when you remember that you will still be map reading and making difficult and rapid decisions about your route after covering several kilometres of rough ground at speed.

A look at the legend (see page 11, fig. 10)

1) Notice the great differentiation between the various types of roads, tracks, paths and rides, according to their size and runnability.

2) Boundaries are given special treatment with uncrossable boundaries being especially important. On some maps, particularly in Scotland, the "stone wall" and the "derelict stone wall" have their own symbols.

3) Contours and topographical detail often show the greatest variation from the Ordnance Survey map. The reason is that orienteers are not solely interested in heights and slopes, but in the recording of almost all mappable features that exist. To extra facilitate this, orienteering maps are increasingly using a 5-metre contour interval as opposed to the O.S. $2\frac{1}{2}$" map contour interval of 25 feet (7.62 metres). Notice the form lines showing kinks in the land occurring between contours, also the knolls, depressions, gullies and boulders which ordinary maps would tend to omit.

Further down the legend, one sees the great differentiation in marshes — crossable or uncrossable, wooded or open, permanent or temporary. And finally, note the variety of open land.

Increasingly also a screen of dots (usually in green) and of varying densities is used to denote the penetrability of the vegetation. This may extend from "Run Easily" to "Fight" (or occasionally on some maps "Jungle").

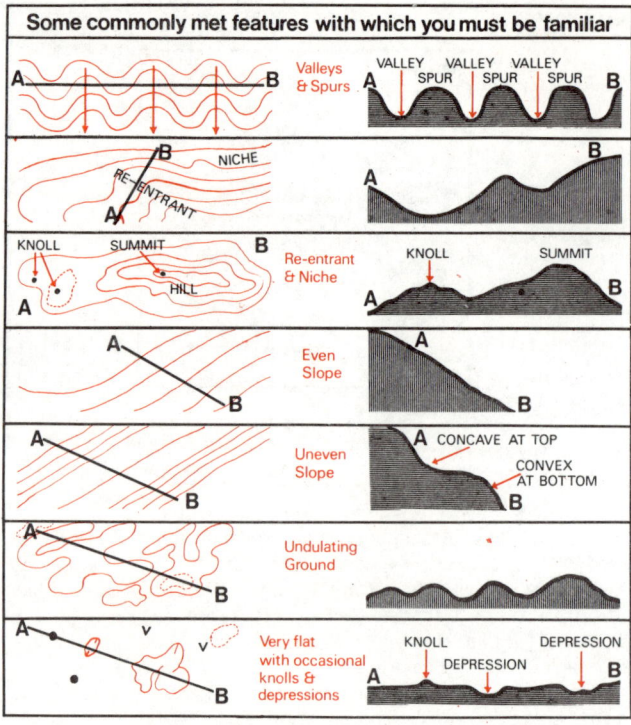

Fig. 7. *By no means represents a comprehensive coverage of all the various contour features likely to be encountered, but it is sufficient for the beginner. As early as possible you must recognise examples in the 'field' and develop the skill of visualising these features in your mind when you see their contour pattern.*

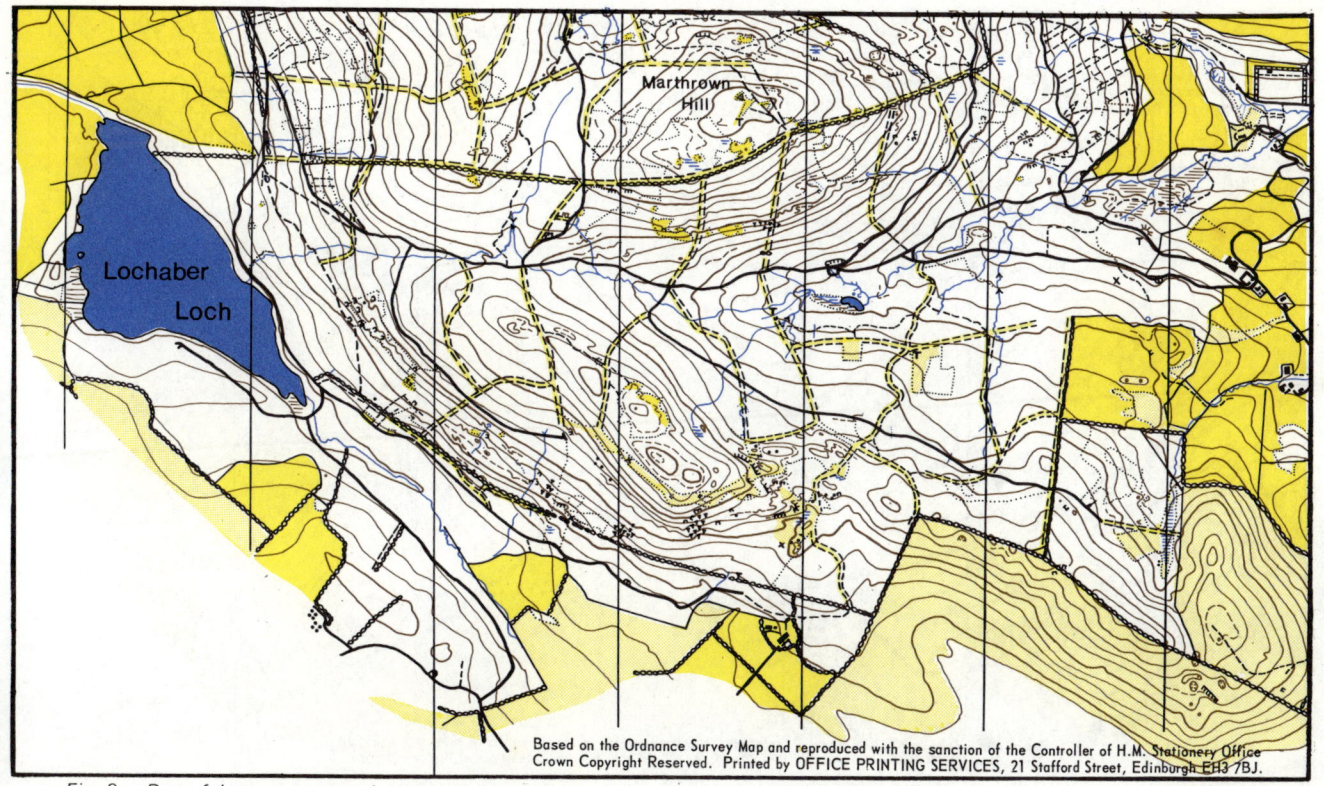

Fig. 8. *Part of the map one receives at registration.*

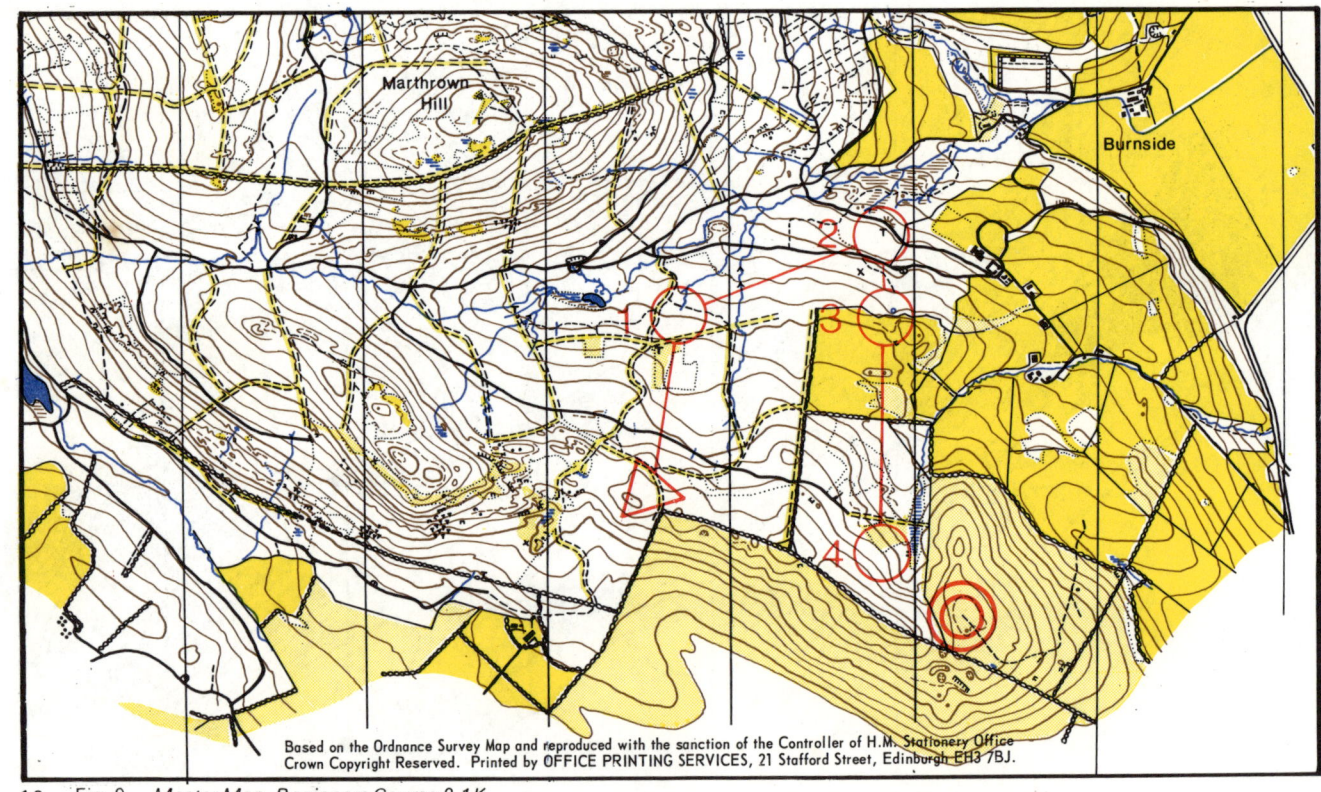

Fig. 9. *Master Map. Beginners Course 2.1K.*

SYMBOLS FOR BRITISH ORIENTEERING MAPS

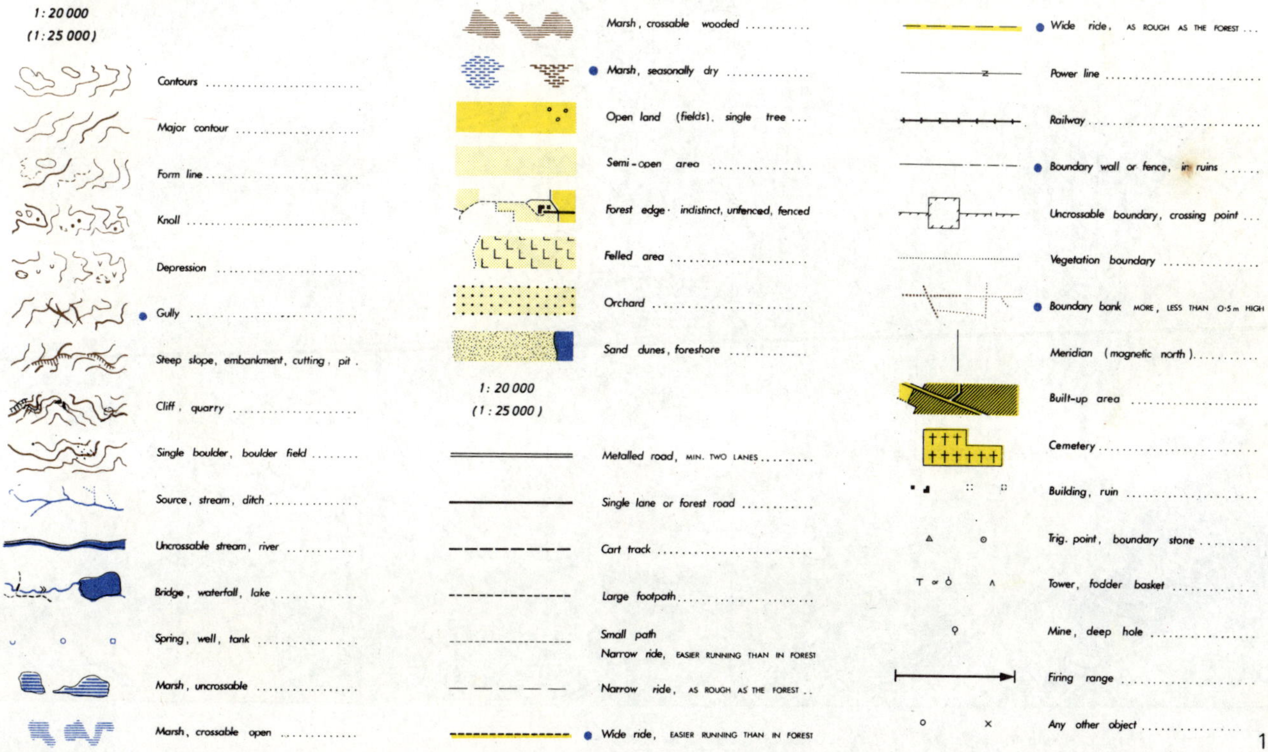

1 : 20 000
(1 : 25 000)

Contours
Major contour
Form line
Knoll
Depression
- Gully
Steep slope, embankment, cutting, pit
Cliff, quarry
Single boulder, boulder field
Source, stream, ditch
Uncrossable stream, river
Bridge, waterfall, lake
Spring, well, tank
Marsh, uncrossable
Marsh, crossable open

Marsh, crossable wooded
- Marsh, seasonally dry
Open land (fields), single tree
Semi-open area
Forest edge - indistinct, unfenced, fenced
Felled area
Orchard
Sand dunes, foreshore

1 : 20 000
(1 : 25 000)

Metalled road, MIN. TWO LANES
Single lane or forest road
Cart track
Large footpath
Small path
Narrow ride, EASIER RUNNING THAN IN FOREST
Narrow ride, AS ROUGH AS THE FOREST
- Wide ride, EASIER RUNNING THAN IN FOREST

- Wide ride, AS ROUGH AS THE FOREST
Power line
Railway
- Boundary wall or fence, in ruins
Uncrossable boundary, crossing point
Vegetation boundary
- Boundary bank MORE, LESS THAN 0.5 m HIGH
Meridian (magnetic north)
Built-up area
Cemetery
Building, ruin
Trig. point, boundary stone
Tower, fodder basket
Mine, deep hole
Firing range
Any other object

Fig. 10.

11

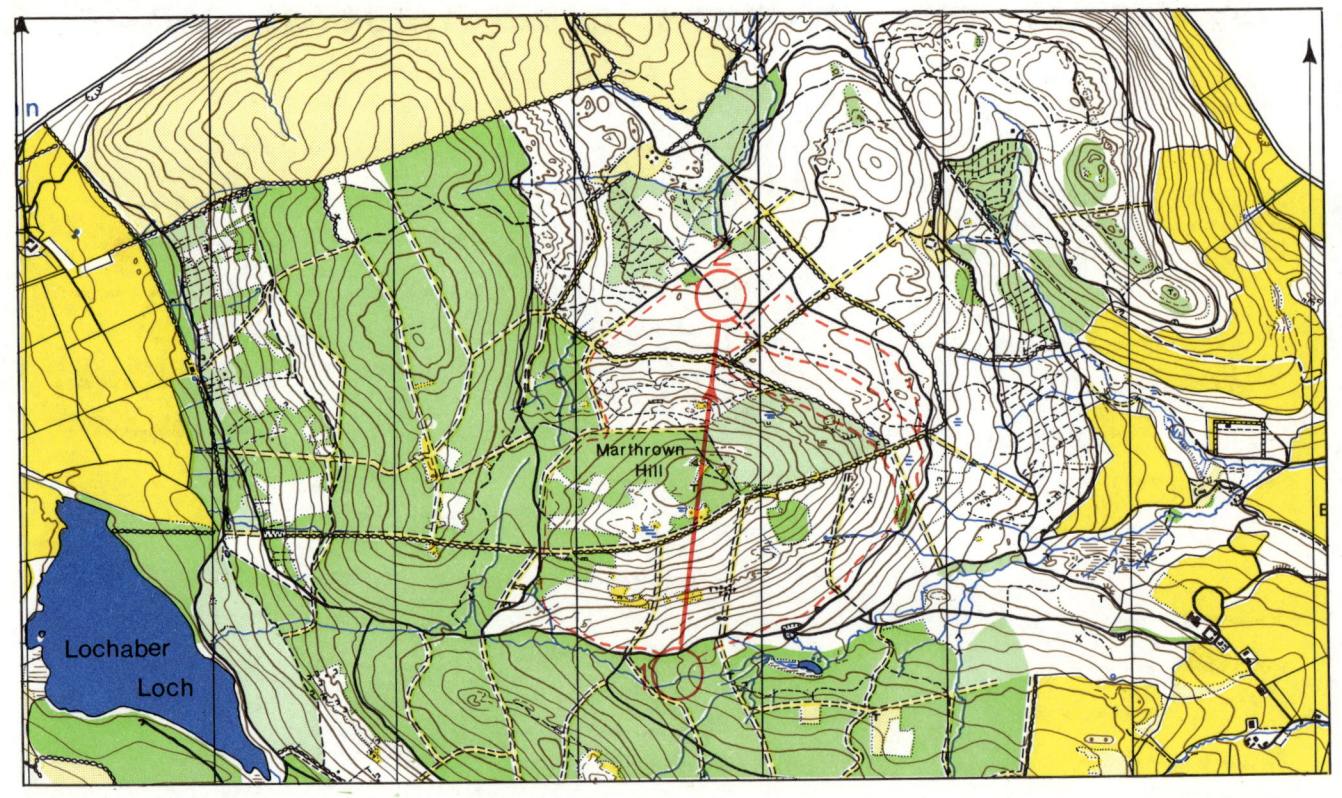

12 Fig. 11. *Route selection problem 1. Up and over or around.*

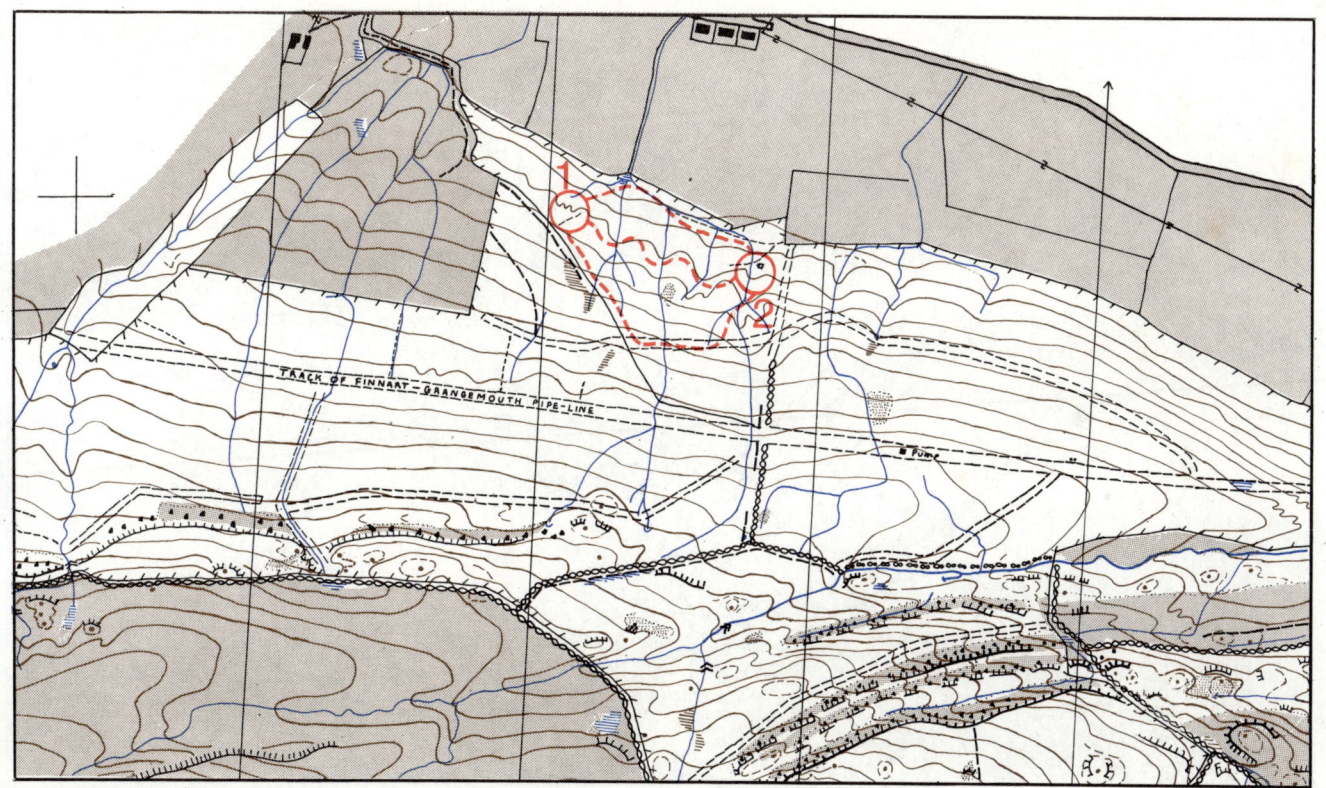

Fig. 12. *Route selection problem 2. 'Contouring'.*

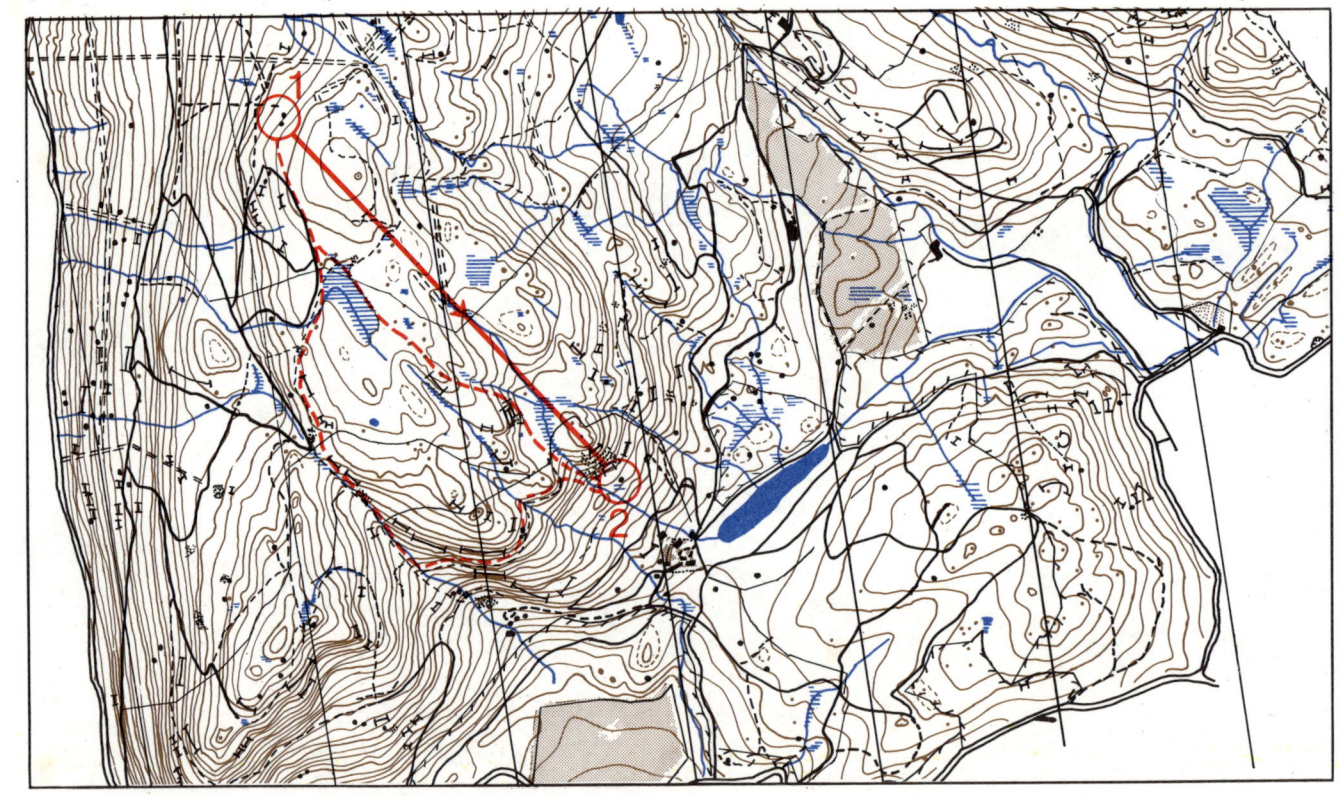

Fig. 13. *Route selection problem 3. Using natural features.*

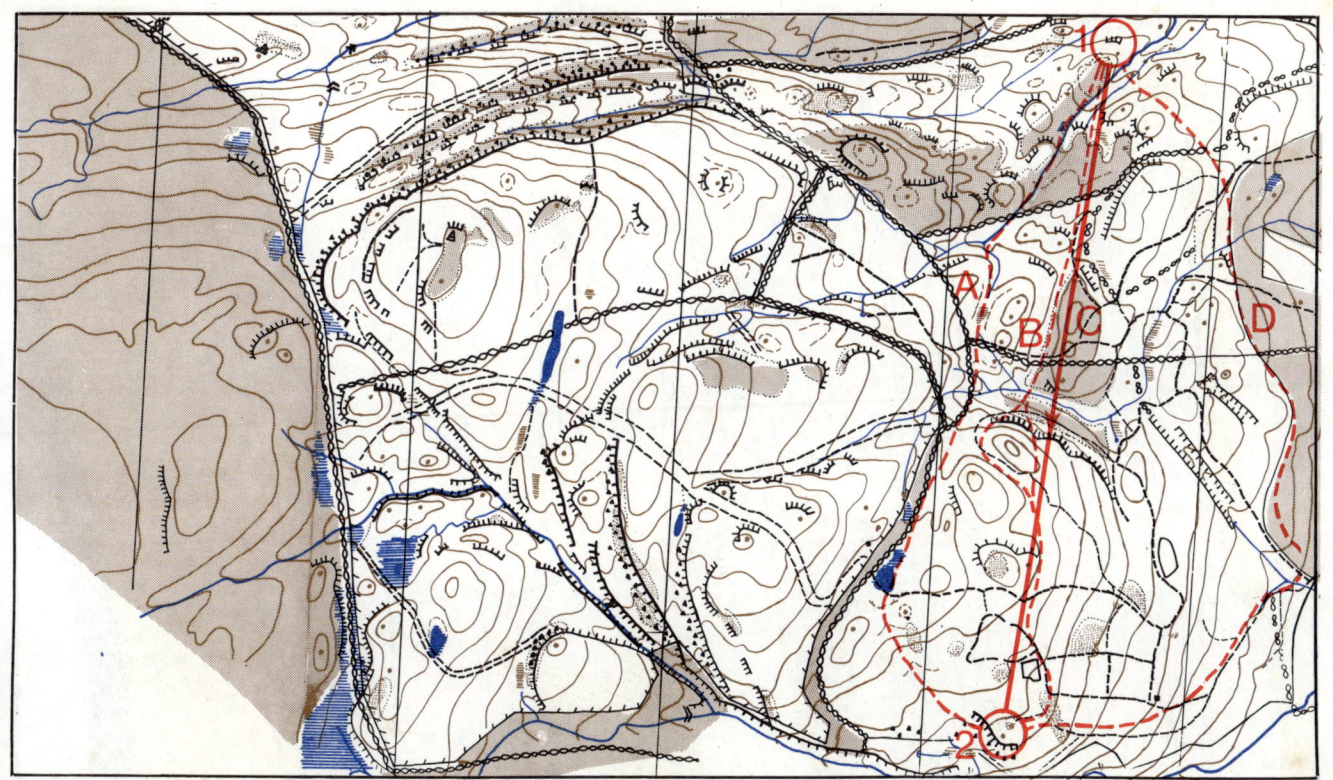

Fig. 14. *Route selection problem 4. The complicated long leg.*

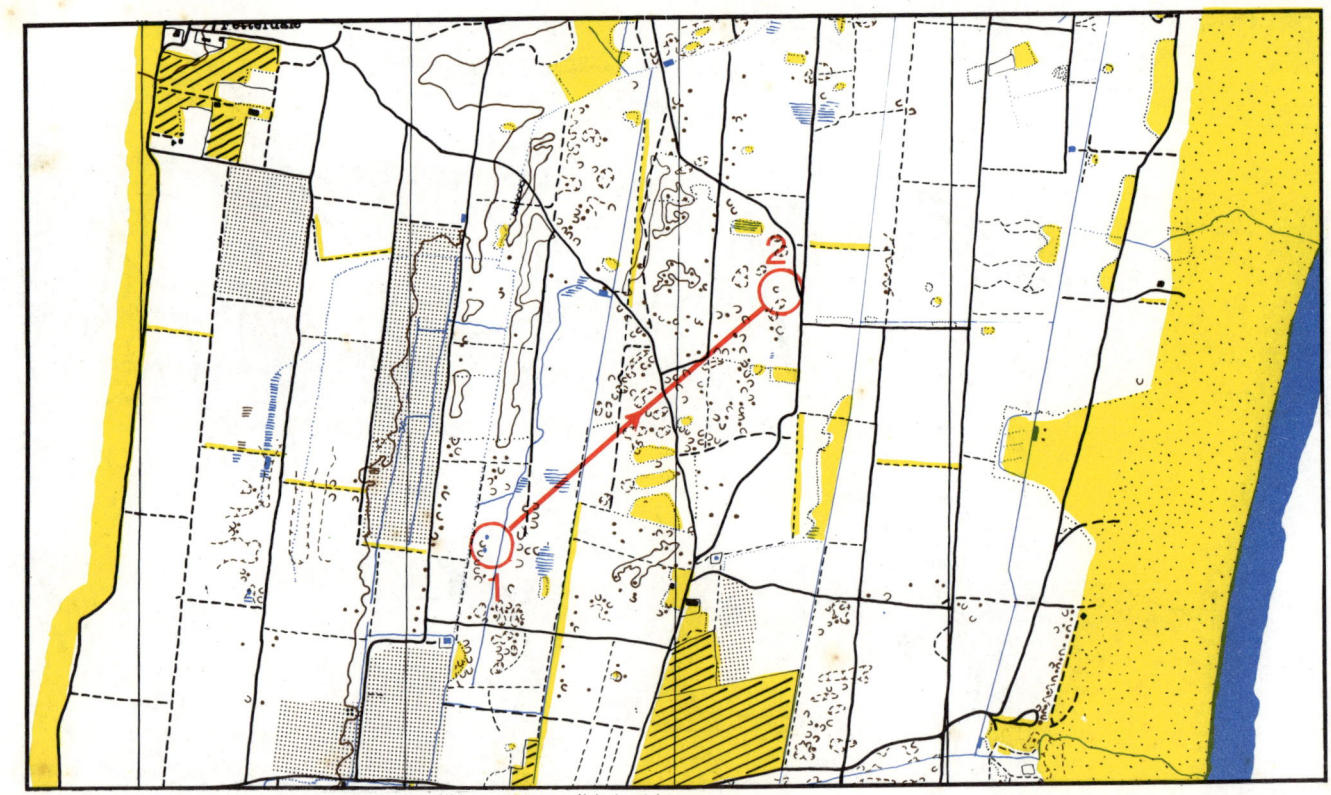
Fig. 15. *A straight, direct approach will be most sensible in this area.*

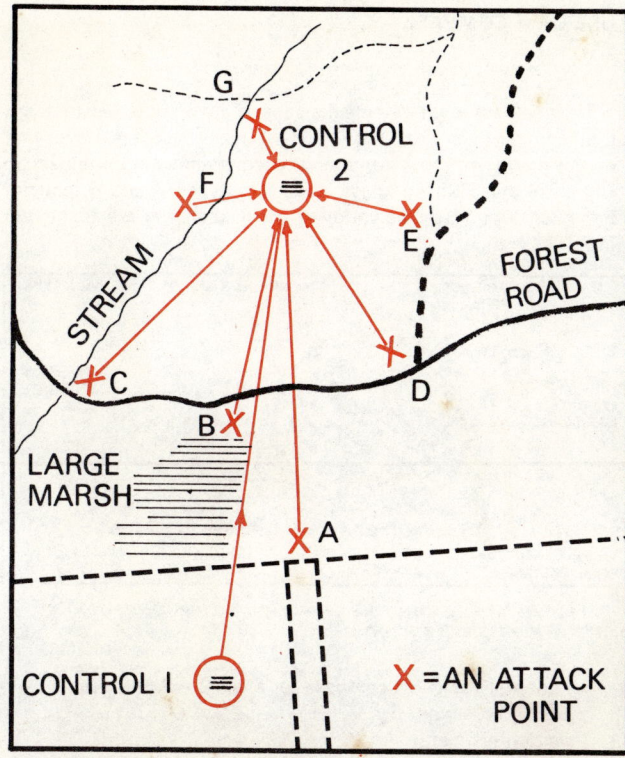

Fig. 16. *Route selection problem 6. Diagram illustrating the variety of 'attack points' available for one control.*

Orienteering Skills

Map Interpretation and Route Selection

Orienteering is based on maps and for the moment we shall ignore the compass. All too frequently beginners get tied up with the compass and forget the map. Orienteering maps are accurate and the beginner's task is to navigate using the *map* and especially to know where he is on the map at all times.

A few of the more common problems you will face on orienteering courses follow.

Some route selection problems

Problem 1 (see page 12, fig. 11) Control 2 is situated on the north side of the hill from Control 1. Which is the best route? Over the top? For the very strong climber the direct route may be best. For others a longer, more gentle route is better. But which side of the hill — east or west, both are equally far? One is downhill at the start, the other uphill. Which is the better route? This is the choice that the orienteer must make.

Problem 2 (see page 13, fig. 12) Controls 1 and 2 are situated at the same height on the same slope. To be safe we might take either the northerly or the southerly route, the latter of which involves an energy wasting climb of 100 feet. Should we save energy and maintain our height, carefully "contouring" along the hillside?

Problem 3 (see page 14, fig. 13) In this example the safe route follows a path running well west and south of the control. A much shorter and more skilfully thought out route depends on the use of natural features. The orienteer heads south until he reaches the forest track, which he follows to the large marsh. He uses the eastern edge of the marsh to guide him onto a small spur which he follows downhill onto another large marsh, the southern edge of which eventually guides him into the control — the boulder at the foot of the scree slope.

Problem 4 (see page 15, fig. 14) This is the "complicated long leg". We could play safe again, by following routes A or D. Though both add distance, each might be a feasible "best route". Indeed D is remarkably flat except for the final few hundred metres and is suitable for fast running. B is very close to the direct line (C) and makes use of a variety of features — the edges of open spaces, paths where they run in approximately the right direction and of course all the time relying on constant knowledge of where one is on the map.

Problem 5 (see page 16, fig. 15) This area is very flat and normally helpful linear features such as paths and tracks run transverse to the particular leg. In this case the best route is almost certainly the straight one, on a compass bearing.

Problem 6 (see page 17, fig. 16) Rarely will an orienteer make his final attack on a control all the way from the previous control. Usually he will orienteer to a much closer and easily recognisable feature and make his attack or final approach from there, usually on a compass bearing. Such features are called "attack points". On fig. 16 the experienced orienteer might attack from A or B whereas the beginner — more cautious and more timid might attack from D or E. To be absolutely safe one might even attack from G. Moreover the orienteer who attacked from A and missed the control would probably use G for his second attack.

USE OF A COMPASS

The compass is the orienteer's second most important tool, but the beginner must not allow its use to take precedence over that of the map. The most commonly used orienteering compass in Britain is the Silva compass, especially types 3 and 4, and for beginners type 7NL. The various parts of the compass are shown in fig. 17.

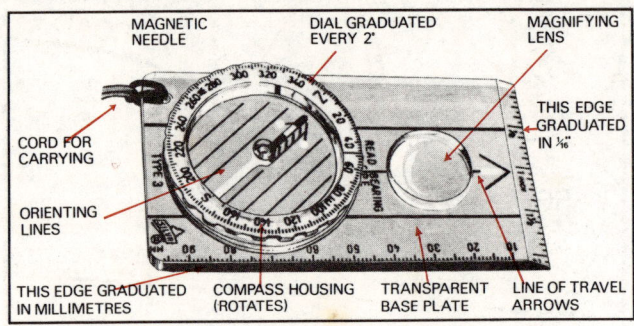

Fig. 17. *All types of compass generally used for orienteering are similar in principle to the above.*

An orienteer uses his compass for a variety of purposes:
    Taking a bearing.
    Setting his map.
    For the final attack.
    For "aiming off".
    For determining position.

Stages in Taking a Compass Bearing

Stage 1 Place the edge of the compass base place along the line of intended travel. Ensure that "line of travel arrow" is pointed in the direction you wish to go (and not 180° in the wrong direction).

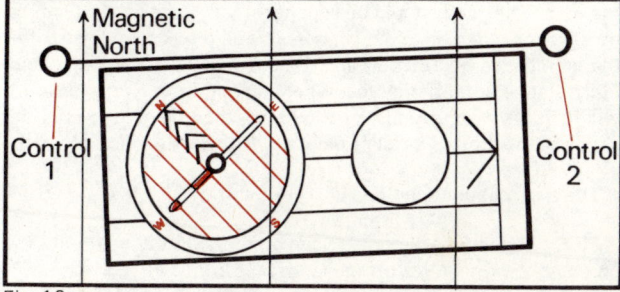

Fig. 18a.

Stage 2 With the map and compass base plate firmly held together, move the compass housing round until the red orienting lines are parallel with the "magnetic north lines" and the orienting "north" points to the top of the map.

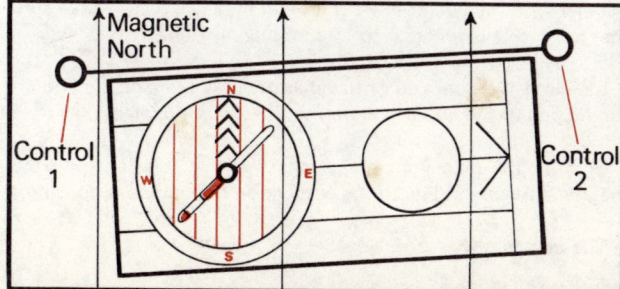

Fig. 18b.

Stage 3 You can now remove your compass from the map. With the compass flat in the palm of your hand, move round bodily until the magnetic needle is pointing to north parallel to the orienting line. The line of travel arrow is now pointing in the actual direction of control 2. As you move off along your bearing take a sighting as far ahead as possible (perhaps on a distant tall tree) this will allow for greater accuracy and will also require you to take your bearings less frequently. In terrain where it is impossible to see far ahead it may be necessary to refer to your compass continuously, constantly ensuring that the orienting lines and magnetic needle stay in line.

The competitive, probably hot and sweaty orienteer is not interested in bearings in terms of actual numbers of degrees but simply as directions shown by the line of travel arrow on his compass. The more arithmetical calculations an orienteer has to make the more likely he is to make mistakes.

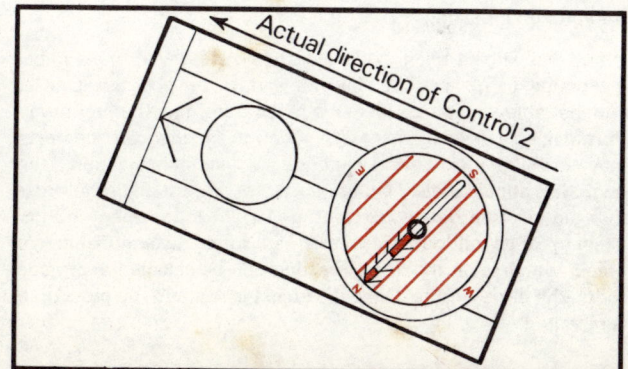

Fig. 18c.

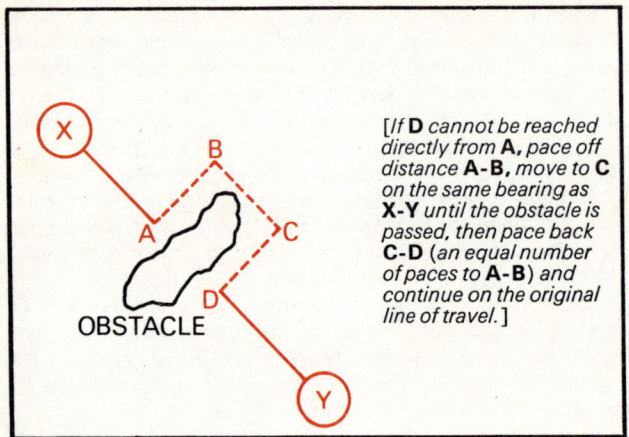

[*If **D** cannot be reached directly from **A**, pace off distance **A-B**, move to **C** on the same bearing as **X-Y** until the obstacle is passed, then pace back **C-D** (an equal number of paces to **A-B**) and continue on the original line of travel.*]

Fig. 19.

Running on a bearing

This has largely been explained above. However, one's initial inclination to go straight may not always be possible. Dense, impenetrable vegetation, perhaps fallen trees, may bar your way thus making a diversion necessary. Though experienced orienteers may develop their own methods of circumnavigation, the beginners should ideally bypass obstacles at right angles in order to maintain true direction. (see fig. 19) In more open country keeping direction becomes easier as some distant distinctive object which is on the line of bearing can be selected and made for by the easiest route. Once the object is reached the procedure is repeated.

Orienting or setting the map

A map is said to be set or oriented when directions on the map correspond to directions on the ground actually represented by the map. The map should be kept constantly set so that it can be quickly consulted as to direction — it is all too easy in the heat of the moment to go 180° off line if the map is being wrongly held. For instance a good orienteer when moving from North to South will read his map upside down! He will then be able to read the shape of the ground as it lies before him on his direction of travel.

The map can be oriented:

1. By aligning easily recognisable points on the map with the corresponding features on the landscape.

2. By means of the compass, using the following drill (see fig. 20).

a) Turn the compass housing until the "orienting lines" are parallel with the line of travel arrow on the base plate. Make sure that north (N) is pointing to "Read Bearing Here".

b) Place the direction of travel arrow on any magnetic line on the map with the arrow pointing to the top of the map.

c) Turn the map with the compass still in position until the magnetic needle points to the N mark on the compass housing.

The map is now set.

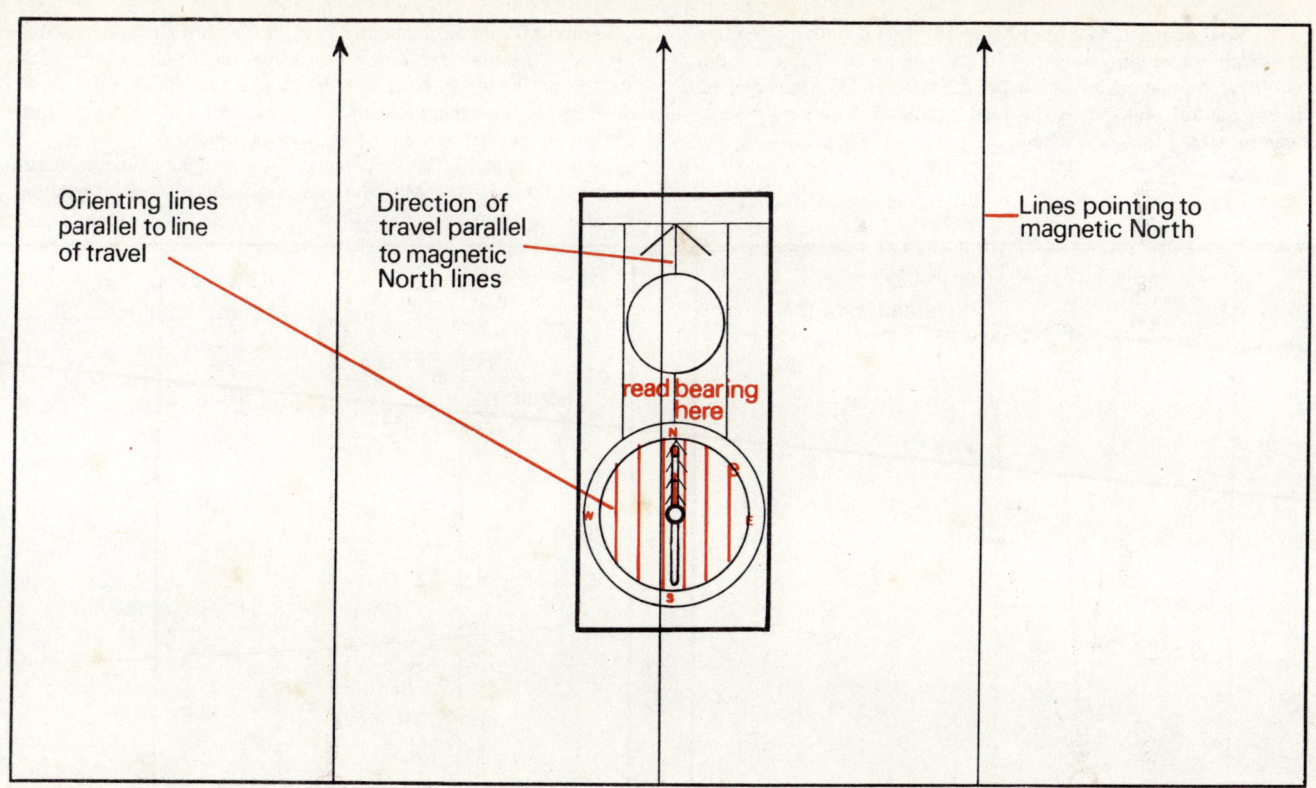

Fig. 20. *Setting the map.*

The final attack (see page 17, fig. 16) This is perhaps the use to which the compass is put most frequently. After having carefully orienteered to within approximately 100 metres or so of the control one makes the final approach on a very precise bearing, taking the utmost care.

Aiming off (see figs. 21a and 21b) This technique is used when a control is situated at a point on some linear feature such as a stream or the edge of a marsh. In fig. 21a the orienteer will deliberately aim either east or west of the control. When he reaches the stream he then knows which way to turn.

Similarly in fig. 21b the orienteer will aim to the marsh edge west of the control. On reaching the marsh he turns right and finds the control.

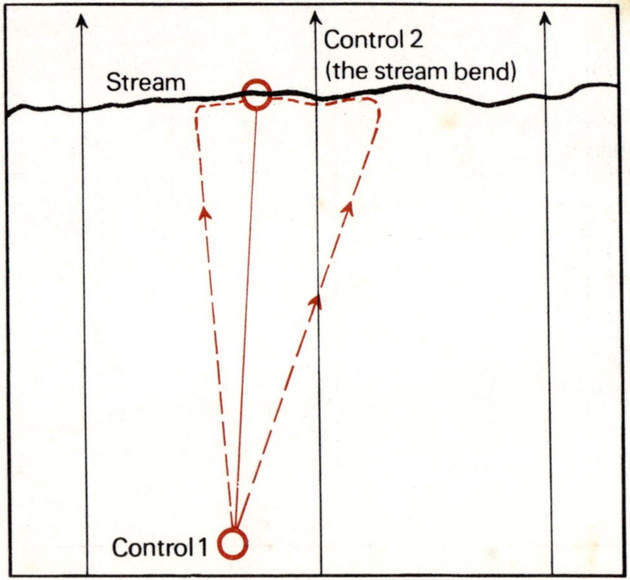

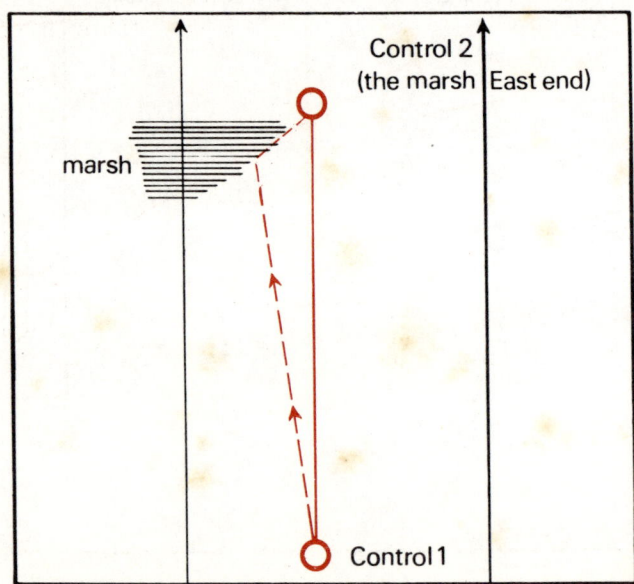

Fig. 21a.

Fig. 21b. *Aiming off.*

Determining position This is a simple procedure for locating one's position on a linear feature such as a stream, ride, path or fence and is shown in figs. 22a and 22b.

While the line of travel arrow is pointed directly at the hill summit the orienteer turns the compass housing until the orienteering lines are parallel with the magnetic needle. The compass is placed on the map as in fig. 22b and the orienteer discovers himself to be located at X.

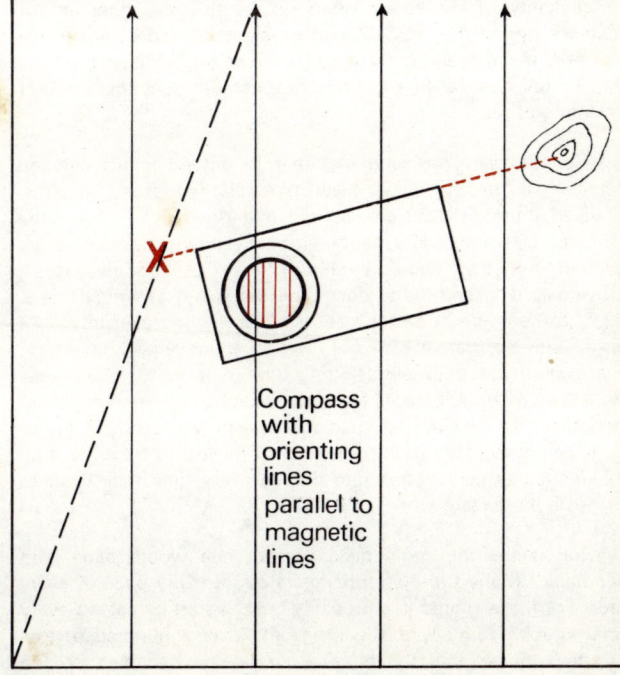

Orienteer knows he is somewhere on this track

Prominent hill which is obvious on the map

Compass with orienting lines parallel to magnetic lines

Fig. 22a.

Fig. 22b.

Measurement of distance

The combination of strange map scales (see fig. 23a) and the unfamiliarity of the forest often makes the misjudgement of distance one of the most difficult problems for the beginner. He can read his map and quickly learns to use his compass but how can he tell how far he's gone? The orienteer does this through counting paces.

It is necessary for each orienteer to determine his average number of running paces over particular surfaces — paths, bracken, through the trees, up hill and down hill — over the standard distance of 100 metres. Normally, orienteers count every second step and therefore talk in terms of "double-paces". Obviously it takes time to determine the speed at which one is likely to compete but after a short while anyone can develop a sufficiently accurate measure of his pace to make his final attack. For example, an orienteer using 45 double paces for 100 metres will take 135 double paces for a final attack of 300 metres. Many orienteers fix their average pacing scale to the leading edge of their compass (see fig. 23b) instead of having to translate from millimetres or centimetres into metres every time they wish to measure the distance.

What is the maximum distance that one would pace with accuracy? Many top class orienteers count every pace of every race. For the beginner it is probably best to start by pacing every final attack. Normally this will be only over a hundred or two hundred metres, but the more accurate one becomes, so the distances will increase.

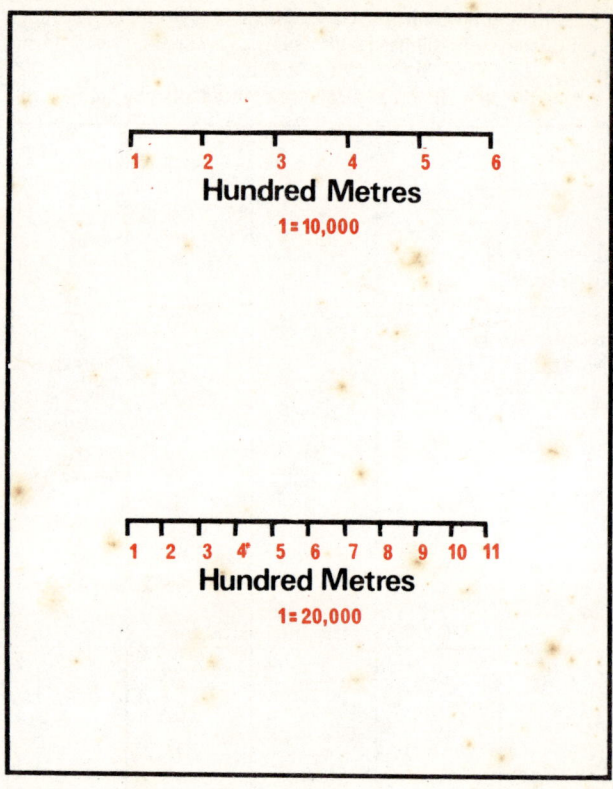

Fig. 23a.

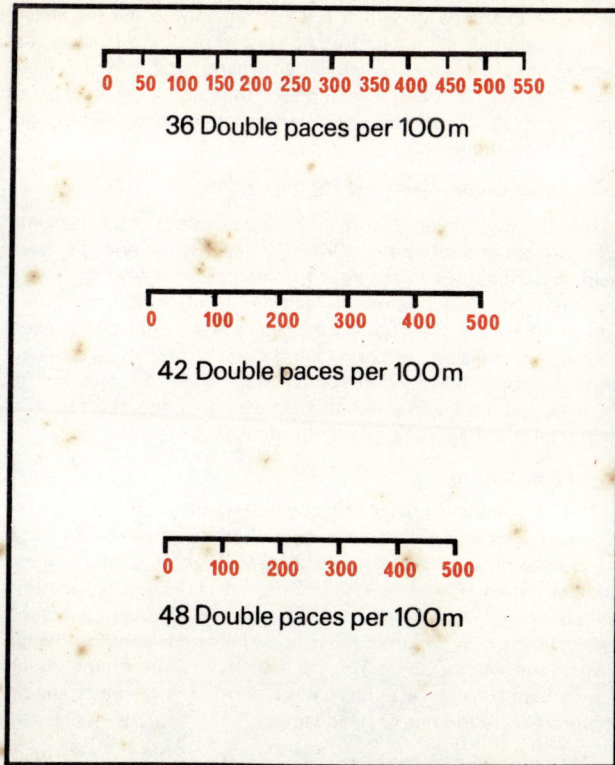

Fig. 23b. *Examples of facing scales for use on maps of 1:20,000 scale.*

Development of "Map-Memory"

For the seriously competitive orienteer any unnecessary waste of time must be avoided. We have considered the necessity to follow the most efficient route, but equally, excessive waste of time looking at the map is unacceptable.

The orienteer must therefore develop the skill of retaining as much of the map in his mind as possible, after each look. The competitor with a photographic memory is in an extremely advantageous position. Training for map-memory is discussed later.

Types of Orienteering

Cross-country orienteering

This is the classical form of orienteering (see page 33, fig. 26) where competitors must visit a set number of controls in a prescribed sequence in order to finish. Cross-country orienteering is the form used in all major championships and allows the course planner the opportunity to set a variety of specific orienteering problems. In major championships maps will usually be pre-marked with controls, start and finish; but in the majority of events, and certainly those for beginners, master maps will be employed.

Score orienteering (see page 34, fig. 27)

The area chosen for this type of competition is dotted with a large number of controls (up to thirty is usual), care being taken to ensure that there are more controls sited than can possibly be visited by any one competitor in the allotted time. The near controls carry a low points value, whilst those at a distance or which are difficult to find (requiring a higher degree of skill) carry a high points value. As with cross-country orienteering competitors almost always participate individually, except for those who are absolute beginners.

Line orienteering (see page 35, fig. 28)

This is used principally for training purposes. Whereas in cross-country orienteering the control positions are displayed on the master map and the choice of route is left entirely to the competitor, in line orienteering the situation is reversed. A line from start to finish is drawn on the master map, which the competitor transcribes to his own map and then seeks to follow meticulously over the ground. At several points along this line controls are sited, the locations of which are known only to the organiser. The competitor will only find a control by following the line. As each control is found the competitor marks its position on his map. The competitor who completes the course in the fastest time, with most controls visited and plotted accurately on his map, is the winner.

Relay orienteering (see page 36, fig. 29)

This is now included in major championships, both national and international. The first British Relay Championships were held in Scotland in 1972. In the normal form of relay there are three runners in each team. All start and finish at the same point (occasionally the first runners may have a different start). Each runner completes a basic cross-country course of perhaps seven or eight controls, the second runner starting as the first runner finishes, and the third runner after the second runner finishes. The final time is the aggregate total for the team of three.

Night orienteering

This is possible with all the above, though in practice cross-country orienteering is usually adopted. In the interests of safety, controls should be closer and the overall length shorter. Much simpler terrain should be chosen and, of course, open country, which would be uninteresting by day, becomes good orienteering ground by night. Controls must be illuminated, either by lamps (which are not too bright) or by the use of Scotch tape which glows readily when a light shines upon it (competitors should therefore carry torches or head lamps).

Becoming a Group or School Leader

The regional secretary of your particular area will be able to offer you a lot of help. It is imperative that one is in touch with the mainstream of orienteering in one's own area. The sort of information which will be so much more easily available and, of course, very necessary if one does keep in touch with the established orienteers would include:
  i Procedures and costs involved in becoming affiliated.
  ii The location and availability of clubs and nearby practising orienteers.
  iii Instructional courses for leaders.
  iv Information on where to obtain lecturers, films and filmstrips.
  v The availability of orienteering maps.

(See page 46.)

Initial requirements

Ideally a group of beginners should be introduced to the sport gradually in a non-competitive situation. The first thing you will need will be a map of an area for this initial practice which may be obtainable from your regional secretary. Quite small areas of rough ground, woodland or perhaps even parkland are suitable for the beginner. It is very important to obtain permission to use a particular area. It will seldom be refused but one must remember that the development of the sport depends very much on the goodwill of landowners — both public and private.

Special clothing is not immediately required and can gradually be acquired as the beginner becomes more efficient. Probably the best compass for the beginner is the Silva Type 7 NL. which costs about £1 and is widely available.

It is best to begin indoors by reading the map. Most people will already have met maps in their geography classes, especially if they are young people. The first things to point out are the special orienteering legend and why orienteering maps tend to be different from Ordnance Survey maps. Then introduce the idea of scale and distance on the map. At this stage it is better to ignore the compass.

The first outing should always be with small groups to enable the beginners to relate the terrain and the general lie of the land to the map. Encourage prediction and commentary as the group walks round a particular area.

The next stage will be to improvise a few controls using painted tin cans, polythene containers or you can use proper markers if you wish. Once the idea of using a map has been satisfactorily instilled in the beginner, set out a short simple course of three or four controls and let the beginners go round in pairs. At this stage success is extremely important. Initial courses should be very easy with controls situated on large easily identifiable features.

The following points must be remembered from the very beginning of orienteering:
1) Always report to the finish whether you complete the course or not.
2) Know and obey the Country Code. Respect other people's property.
3) Keep quiet in the forest.
4) Try not to follow the man in front. He may be going in the wrong direction.

The Compass

This should be introduced only after a fair amount of practice using only the map. Early lessons can be indoors or on a sports field. Then one can go on to tackle some of the more common orienteering problems.

Before their first event, beginners should be made aware of normal competition organisation — registration, the pre-start, master maps, etc. and especially the following:
1) Safety measures, including a safety bearing if one is given.
2) Map corrections, especially those showing dangerous areas.
3) The latest finishing time (especially important in winter).

After early events it is useful to discuss beginners' successes and their mistakes. Many very experienced orienteers maintain a record of every single error they make, and in their training try to iron out the most frequent ones.

Very early on in one's orienteering career, it will be found that transport is very necessary. Many events are in remote areas so many schools and clubs use mini-buses while others organise a fleet of private cars to help them get to and from the orienteering area.

Training points — The development of orienteering skills

The following training points are designed to improve the performance of the orienteer by guiding the development of the most important skills.

1. Physical fitness.

2. Map memory.

3. Pacing and compass bearing.

4. Line orienteering.

5. Strip orienteering — to encourage the direct approach.

6. Orienteering without a compass.

7. Following a marked route and drawing the route on to a map.

Physical fitness

One of the attractions of orienteering is that it is a sport almost equally attractive to the old as the young, and to the runner as to the walker. But, as with all competitive sports at their highest level, orienteering demands superb fitness and running ability.

This is not the place to describe detailed physical training schedules. It is enough to say that prior to any real orienteering success one requires a considerable background of the sort of training undertaken by a distance runner.

Map memory

The orienteer can greatly assist his skill in retaining the map in his mind by simply deliberately referring to it as little as possible, remembering of course that there is always the danger that a saving of time might well result in increased mistakes.

A useful training race can be employed where "competitors" are not given maps of their own. Instead, at the start and at each subsequent control there are portions of the map showing the next leg. The orienteer is allowed as much time as he requires looking at the map, but then must orienteer to the control using only what he retains in his mind. (see page 37, fig. 30)

Pacing and compass bearing

Controls are set out as for a cross-country orienteering race. Around each control a circular portion of the map is cut out, and these are pasted on to a card in their proper relative places (see page 38, fig. 31). Magnetic lines are added to the card which may then either be used by individuals or may be photocopied. The orienteer must navigate between the controls by compass and by pacing. For beginners, the map circles can be made relatively large, but can be made small for the relatively experienced competitors. A more advanced alternative to this is not to use maps at all, but simply to offer the course as a series of distances and compass bearings.

Line orienteering

Line orienteering encourages the orienteer to know exactly where he is all the time, and is therefore very useful for training. As you become more proficient, your "lines" should have their bends increasingly in indeterminate places, away from tracks, stream bends and the like. (see page 35, fig. 28)

Strip orienteering

The majority of top orienteers run as straight as possible between controls, and the fitter one becomes the more possible this is.

To encourage the direct approach, set out a normal cross-country course, but supply only narrow strips of the map. (see page 39, fig. 32) "Competitors" will be able to vary from the "straight and narrow" only very slightly.

Orienteering without a compass

This is most valuable training at all levels ; to bring home the fact that good map-reading is the fundamental skill of orienteering.

Following a marked route

A route may be set out in the forest using streamers. Orienteers are sent along the route — beginners can walk ; experienced competitors must run — and on their return must record the exact route followed by the streamers. Controls may be set along the route as with line orienteering.

Obviously all the above are basic methods which can be used at almost all levels — depending on the terrain used, the distances involved and the general difficulty of orienteering.

PART 2
Competitions and Organisation

Preparing for a competition

As this booklet is primarily for the beginner, it is not the right place to go into the amount of detail on organisation which would be required for a major championship. Nevertheless, the fundamental principles remain the same throughout the various levels of competition and the lessons which it is necessary to learn will stand one in good stead for later, more advanced events. We shall assume that you, the beginner, will eventually organise an event on the level of an open club competition.

All competitions should have the following basic group of officials:

- Course planner
- Controller
- Organiser
- Map maker(s) (if a new map is necessary).

The Course planner

The Course planner is responsible for choosing the area, for planning the courses and for the siting of the controls. The task is by no means easy. Unused forests are certainly difficult to find in many areas. A new club event might well have to make do initially with an inferior area.

Courses must be fair, must offer a variety of orienteering problems, and always a variety of route choice. They must be the right length according to the class of competition, the terrain, the vegetation and the time of year. For example, senior men may expect to finish in 70 or 80 minutes, but beginners ought to complete their course in 30 minutes or so. The sort of questions the course planner ought to ask himself include "how many controls?" and "how should the balance be made between long legs and short legs?"

Controls should not be hidden. Orienteering is not hide and seek nor is it treasure-hunting. Equally controls should not be high in the branches of trees and be visible for miles. They should be visible from approximately 25 metres. Siting of the start, the master maps and the finish are all the planner's responsibility.

The Controller

The Controller has ultimate responsibility for the courses. He is the double-check on the work of the planner. Normally he is an experienced orienteer. He will be responsible for checking the accuracy of control placing, accuracy of control descriptions, fairness of controls and of each leg, and for safety generally. He may ask for a control to be changed because of dangerous cliffs, or for a course to be shortened because of winter weather or for cancelling the event because of snow.

The Organiser

The Organiser is the event administrator, and in the case of open events is responsible to the B.O.F. for general organisation. He does all the organising other than that involved on the courses, provides all the material requirements for the event and deals with all the correspondence.

Some of his duties might include such things as correspondence with the regional forestry liaison officer, correspondence with police, landowners and with the regional secretary re events in the fixtures list.

He might also be expected to send prior information to competitors; deal with entry forms (though it is most likely entries would be received for this standard of event on the actual day); procure control markers, control punches, control cards; start and finish banners; clocks and watches and description sheets; be responsible for the first aid arrangements and have a doctor on

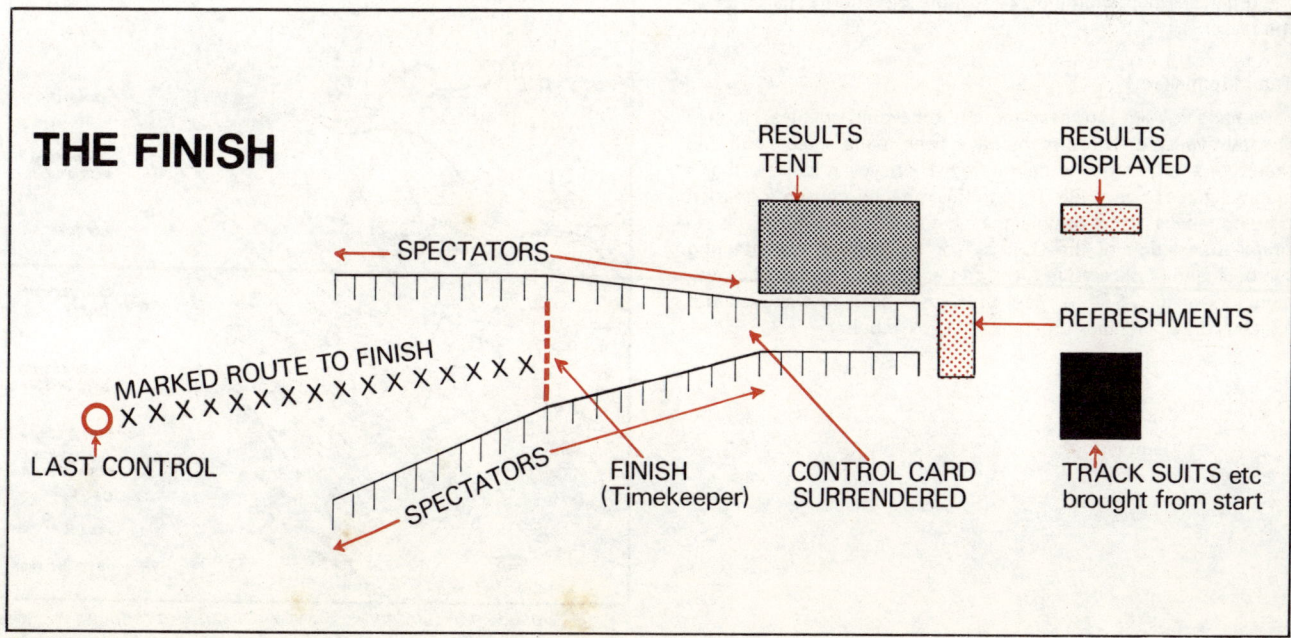

Fig. 24.

call; organise a standby search party; procure sufficient officials for all the various tasks; and to organise trophies, certificates, etc.

After the event he should send out results and letters of thanks. This job is obviously a very large one and must be shared, with various tasks delegated to other members of the club. However, the organiser must ultimately be responsible and in charge of all the tasks.

The Map maker

Perhaps you are fortunate enough to have an orienteering map already available. These maps have been made since 1968 and therefore a large stock is developing. However, it is likely that a map will have to be made. Though this is a time-consuming task it is by no means an impossible one even for the beginner. Even the simple translation of the O.S. 2½" or 6" map into orienteering symbols, and duplicated in black and white is a decided improvement. (See fig. 25 — a map which has been re-surveyed but which is drawn in black and white I.O.F. symbols.)

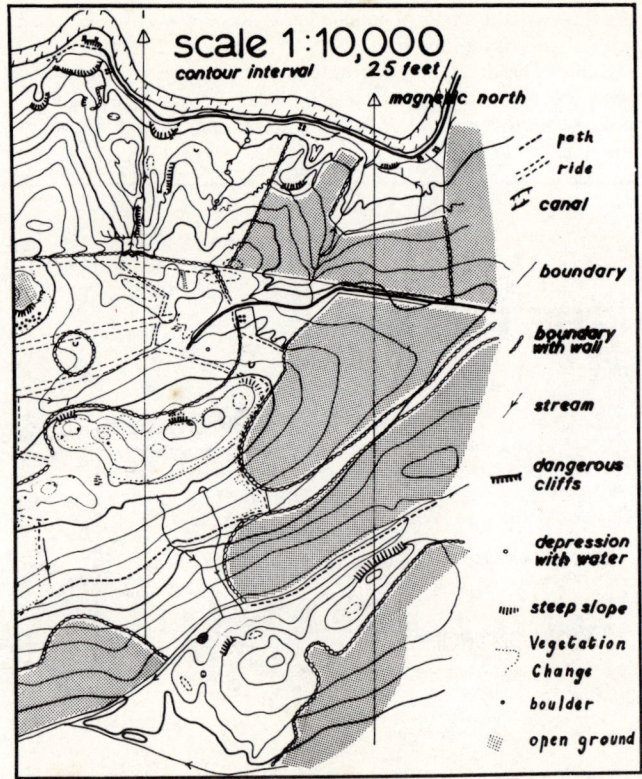

Fig. 25. *Based on the Ordnance Survey Map and reproduced with the sanction of the Controller of H.M.S.O. Crown Copyright Reserved. Printed by Office Printing Services, 21 Stafford Street, Edinburgh.*

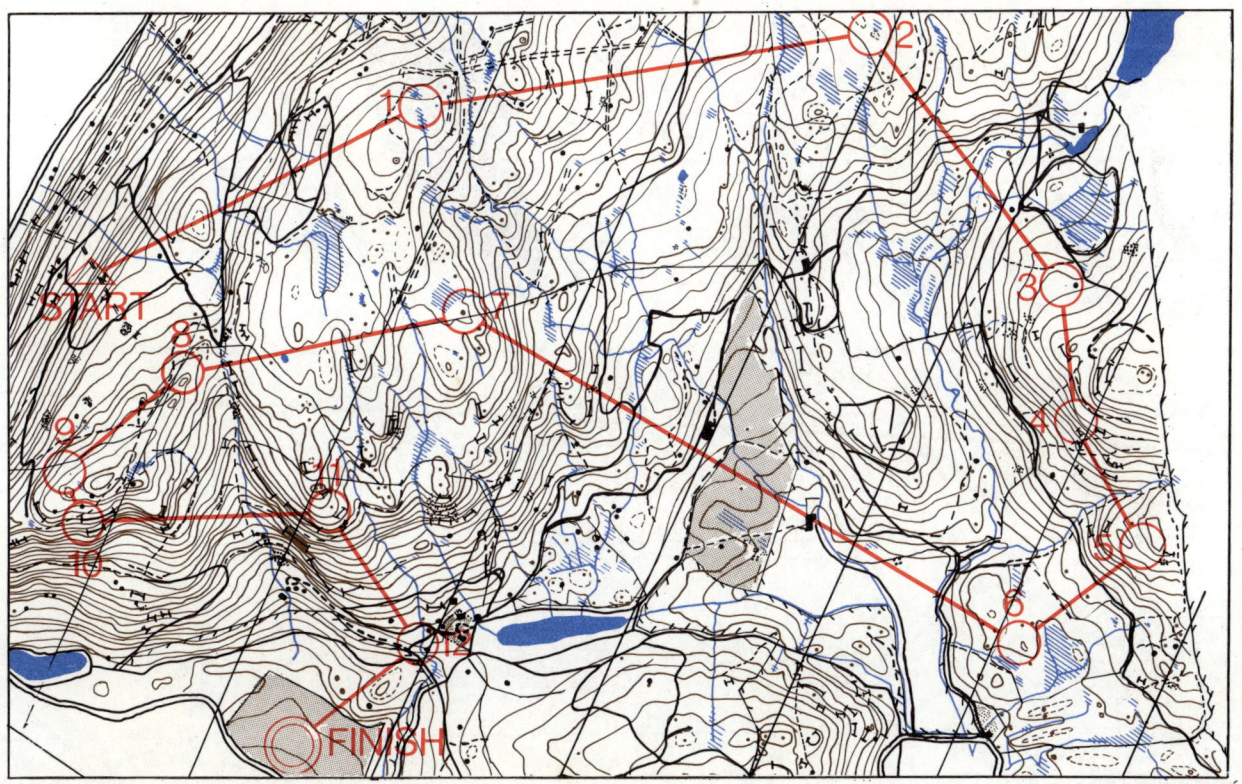

Fig. 26. *A cross country orienteering event.*

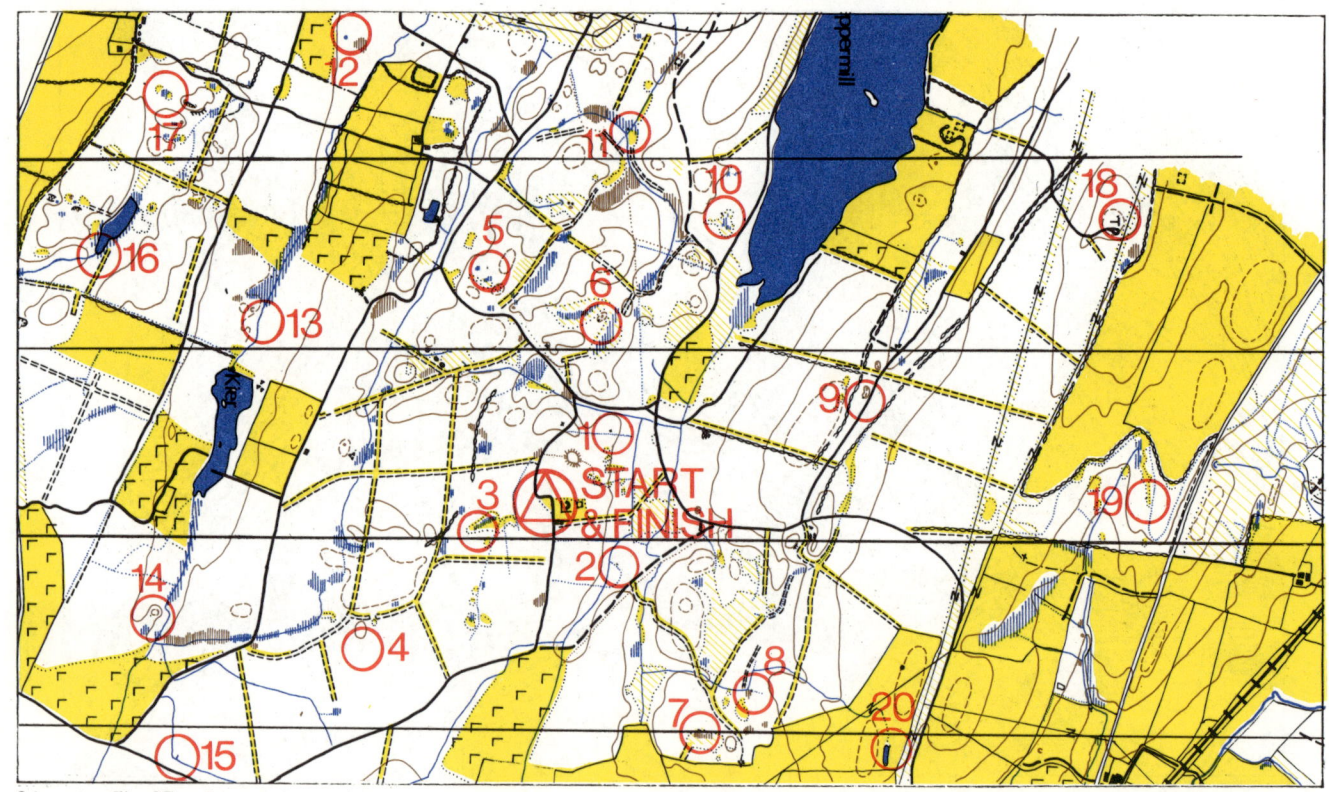

Fig. 27. *Score orienteering.*

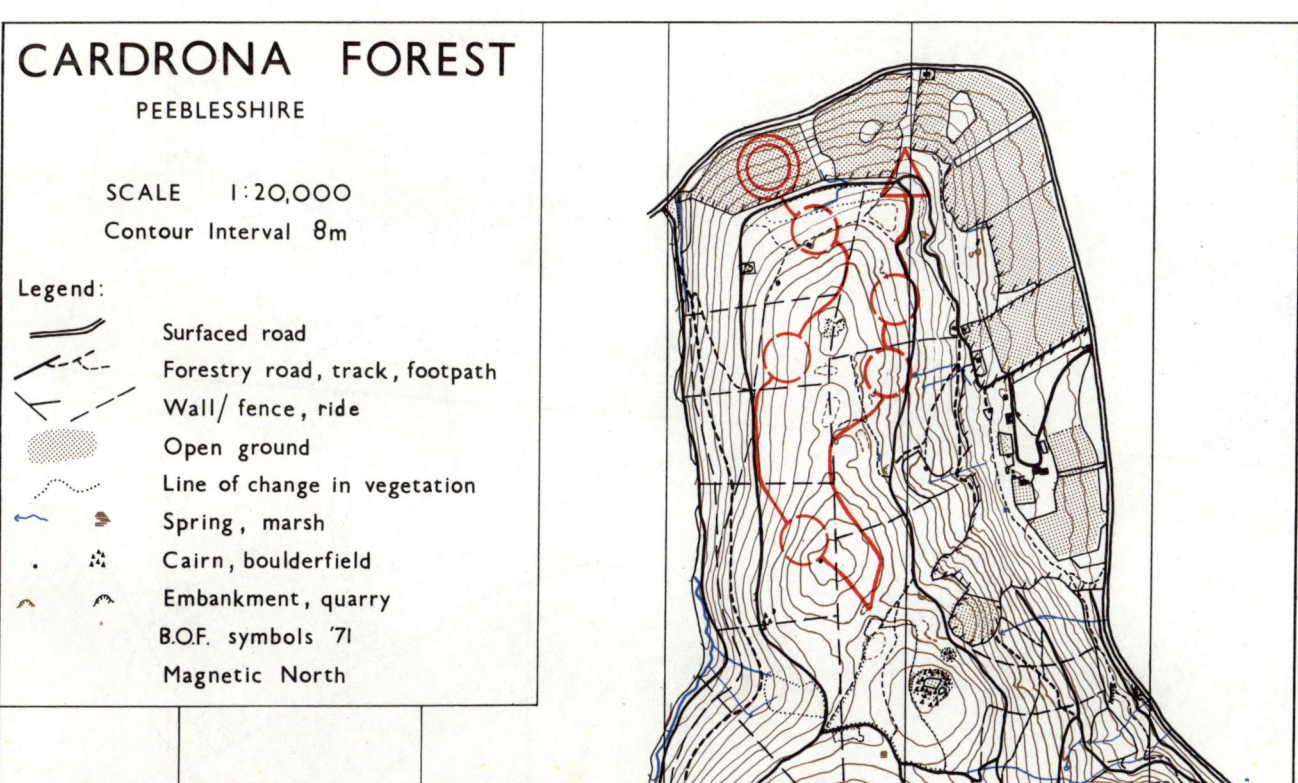

Fig. 28. *A simple line event with controls along the route but not shown on master maps.*

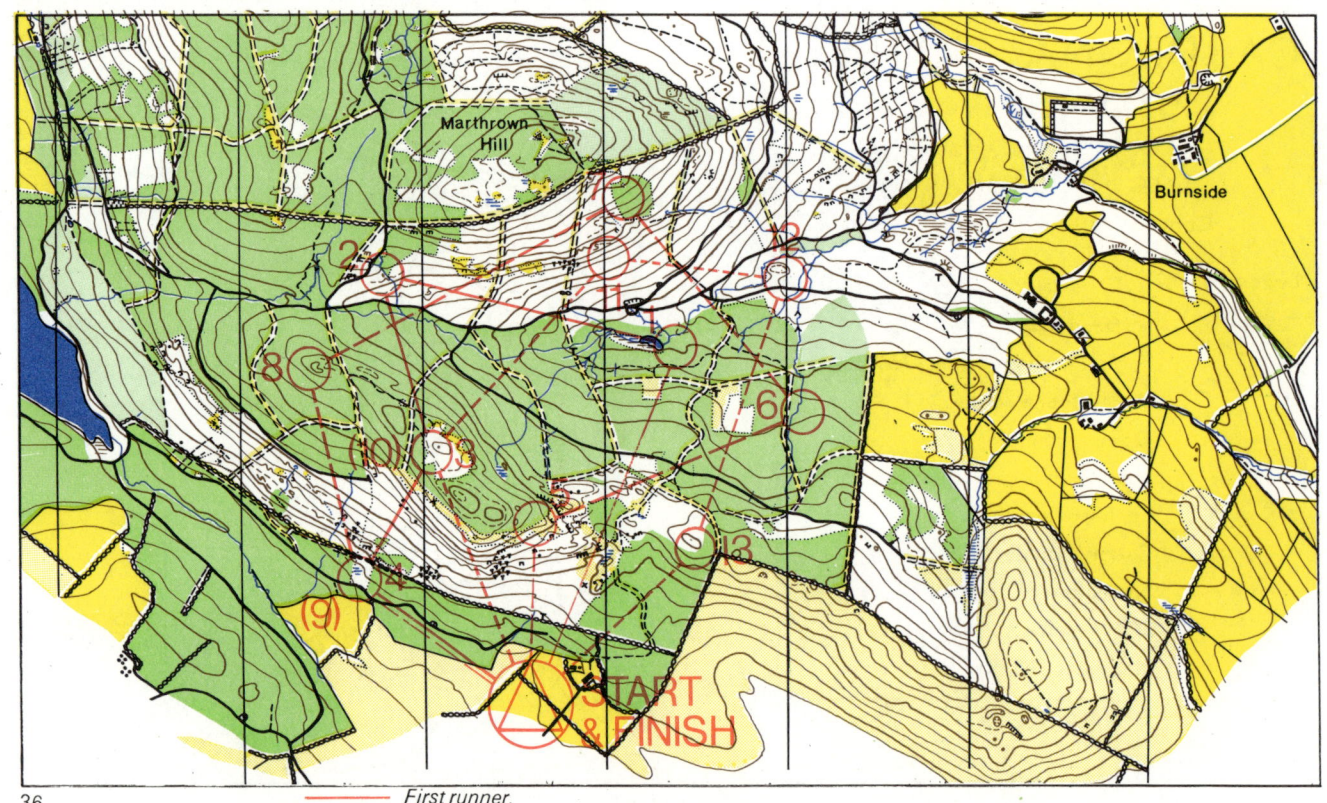

Fig. 29. *A relay course* ——— *First runner.*
— — — *Second Runner.*
- - - - *Third Runner.*

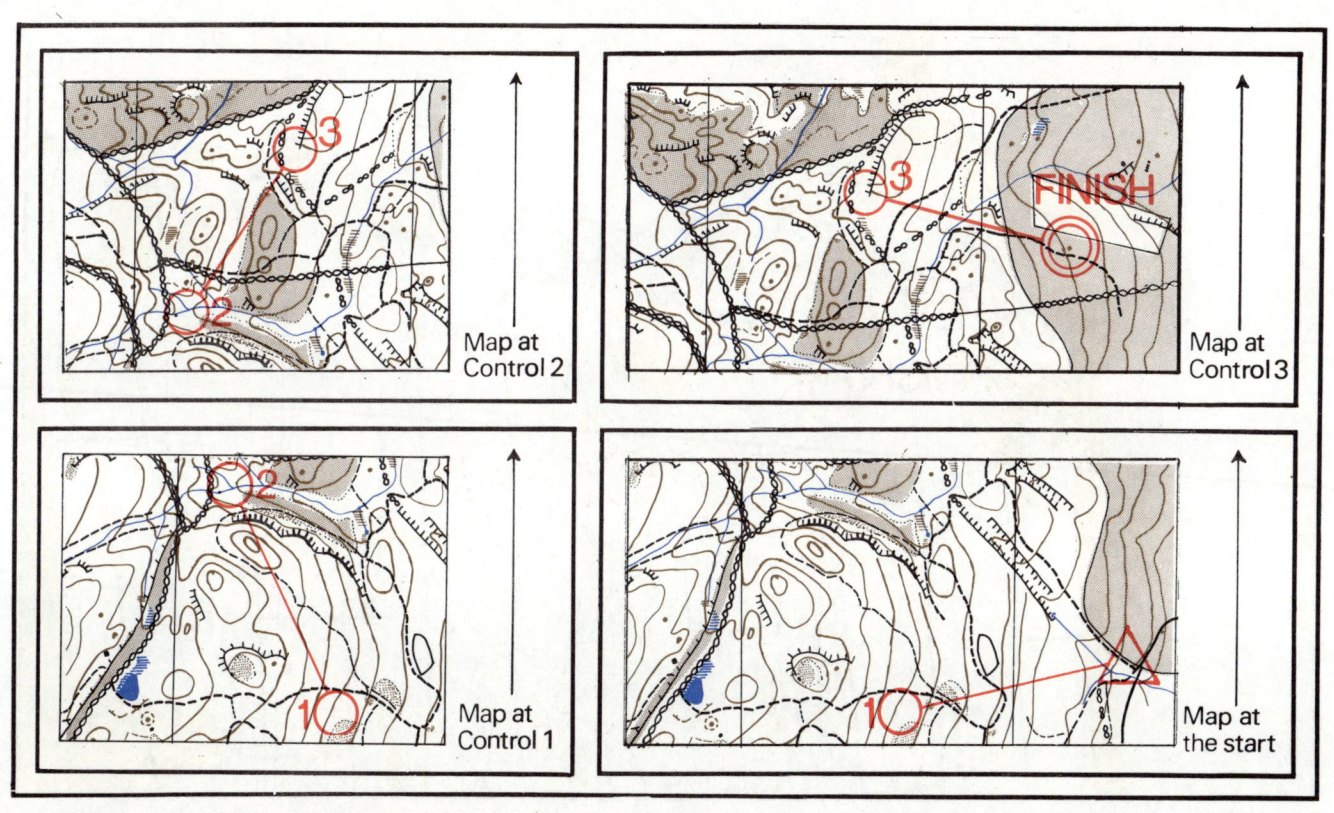

Fig. 30. *The sections of map used in a simple course to develop 'Map Memory'.*

37

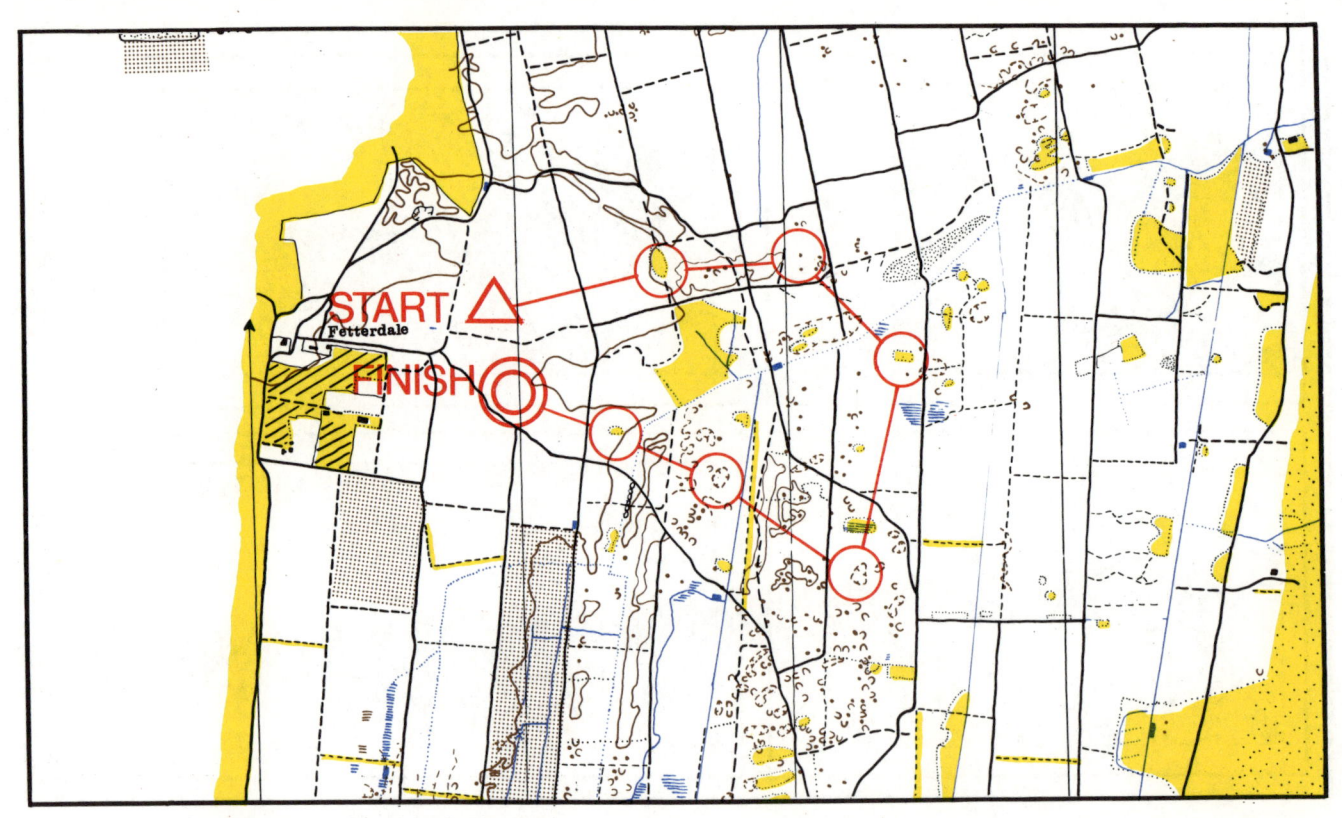

Fig. 31. *Training course for practising pacing work.*

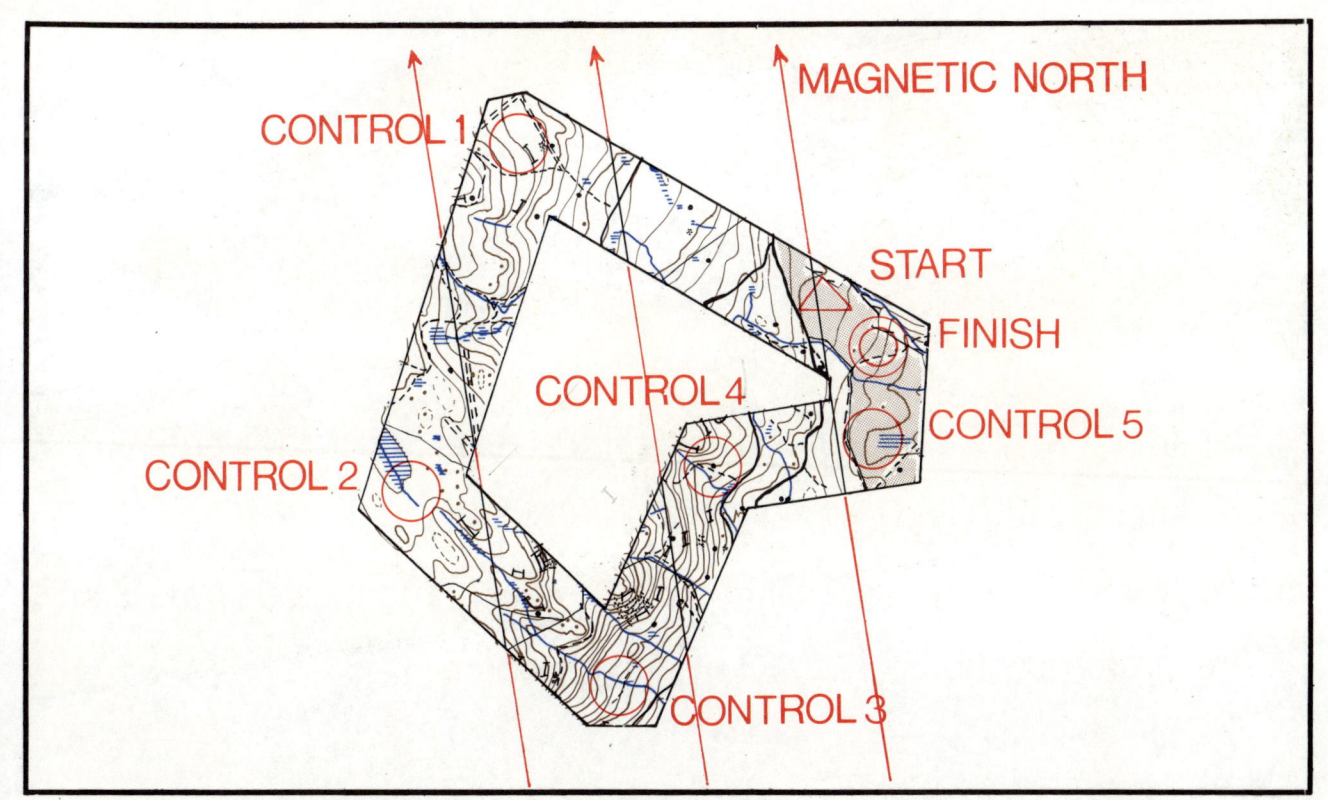

Fig. 32. *Orienteering on strips of the map to encourage a straight approach.*

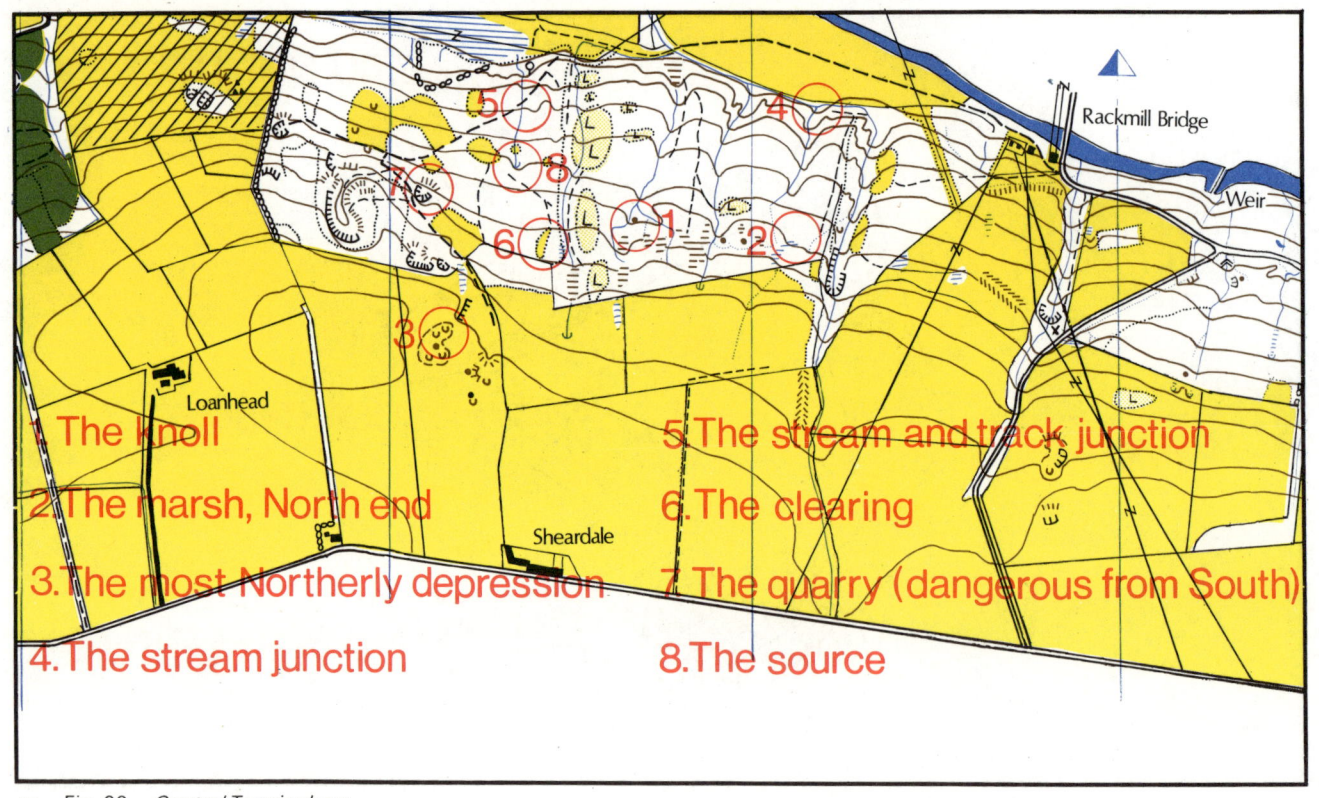

1. The knoll
2. The marsh, North end
3. The most Northerly depression
4. The stream junction
5. The stream and track junction
6. The clearing
7. The quarry (dangerous from South)
8. The source

40   Fig. 33.   *Control Terminology.*

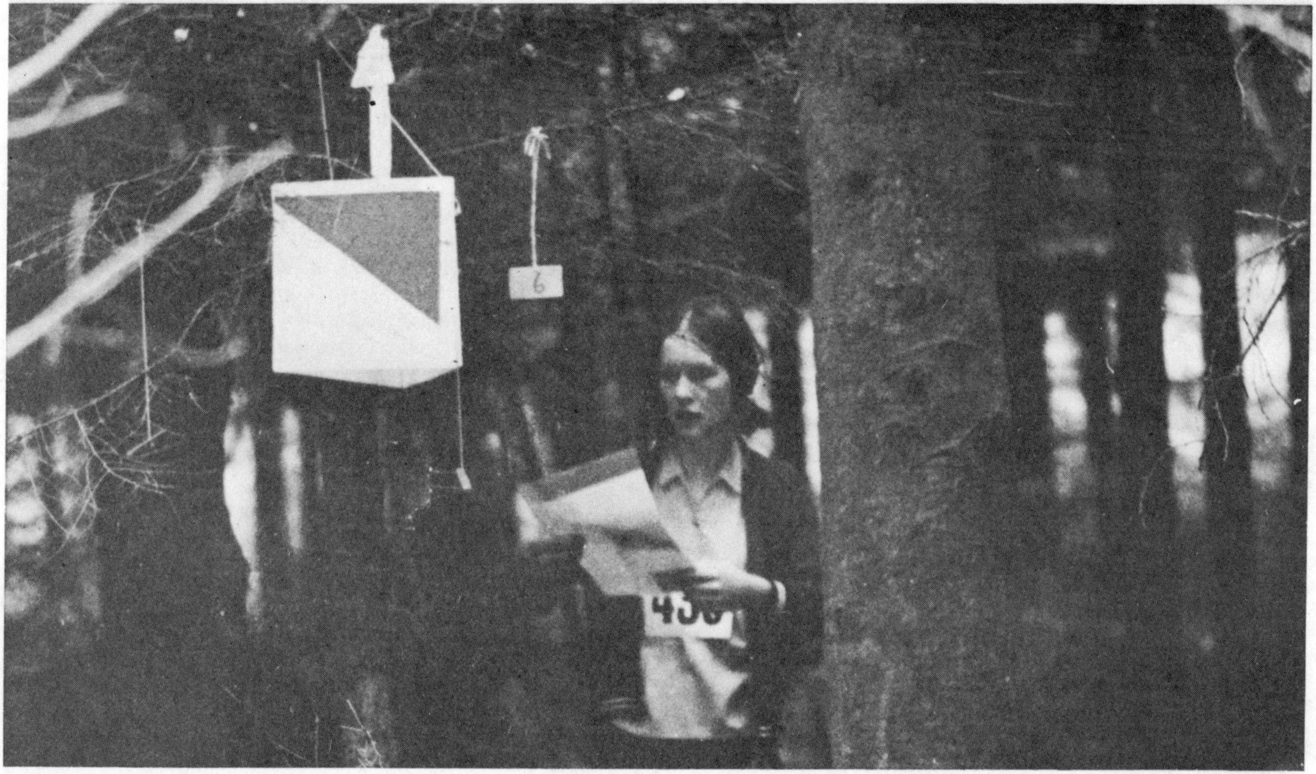
6

TIME-TABLE FOR AN OPEN CLUB EVENT

Up to nine months ahead

a) The main officials must be appointed.
b) The area must be chosen.
c) Permission must be sought from private landowners or Forestry Commission.
d) If there is a map of the area already available then there will probably be no need to resurvey. If there is no map available then map-makers must be appointed.
e) The map must be drawn.
f) The information about the event must be given to "The Orienteer" (B.O.F. monthly magazine), informing fixtures secretary and finding a suitable date.
g) Outline planning should be done; especially to establish start and finish and any information which may help the mappers.
h) The Planner and Controller should do other outline checking, for example identifying any specific problems; out of bounds areas; specific dangers, etc.

One month in advance

a) Other officials should be appointed for registration, start, finish, results, refreshments, traffic, manning of controls, nominating of search team.
b) The map should be printed.
c) Arrangements should be made for having first aid and a doctor on standby.
d) Trophies and certificates should be organised.
e) The courses should be planned.
f) The controlling of the courses should be seen to.

One week ahead

a) Entries should be closed (though prior entries may not be necessary).
b) The master maps drawn up and checked by the controller.
c) The Control Description is produced together with any map corrections.
d) Other materials must be amassed — control markers, start and finish banners, competition cards, etc.

The day before

The control Markers are placed in position.

The day of the event

a) The controller makes the final checks
b) There is a final briefing of officials, positioning of officials and relevant notices and signs.
c) The results are displayed.
d) Trophies are awarded.

After the event

a) Results are posted.
b) Thanks are sent to all who helped.
c) De-briefing — any lessons to be learned.

Safety

Safety is the ultimate responsibility of the Controller. The following precautions should be observed.

The controller must observe:

a) that all competitors are informed of any potentially dangerous areas. Normally this will be done on the "map corrections".

b) that all beginners' courses are kept well clear of areas of potential danger.

c) that in the beginners' events there should be, if possible, a safety bearing which will lead those who are lost "back to civilisation".

d) that all competitors know the "final return time". Normally this will be expressed as "the time at which the final control will be removed".

Also:

e) all competitors must report to the finish whether they have completed the course or not.

f) some organisers require that all competitors carry whistles and that they are familiar with the international distress call.

Control terminology (See page 40, fig. 33)

Control markers are situated on precise features which normally are shown clearly on the map. (In early orienteering, features used as controls were often not shown on the map.)

The control markers must not be hidden. Normally they will be visible from at least 25 metres.

Avoid use of control features which may cause confusion, e.g. a depression located within a few metres of other depressions. If you must do this the control description must clearly distinguish the control, e.g. "the most northerly depression".

Each control will be marked with a letter or number which will be shown on the control description sheet.

Map Making

This booklet is not the place for a comprehensive description of how to make an orienteering map. The B.O.F. booklet "The production of orienteering maps" gives a complete guide. However, there is room to suggest (i) the levels of sophistication of the task and (ii) the basic materials required.

(i) **Levels of sophistication:**

a) The simple translation of O.S. map (2½" or 6") into I.O.F. symbols is the easiest stage, but remember that any reproduction of O.S. maps or production of maps based on O.S. maps requires H.M. Stationery Office permission. Some field checking will be required but no surveying. The resulting maps may be produced in various ways in black and white.

b) Limited field work of perhaps 10 to 15 hours could satisfactorily up-date your black and white map, depending on its area. Fallen trees, new plantation, new fences, new roads can be shown. Moreover, obvious contour errors can be rudimentarily corrected and small features such as knolls and depressions added.

c) Further field work may make it worthwhile to produce a coloured map.

Aerial photographs and their simple interpretation with the use of a pocket stereoscope can greatly assist in all of the above.

(ii) **Mapping materials:**

a) You will need a set of drawing pens ranging from 0.1mm to 1.0mm (e.g. Rotring or Mars Staedtler available from art and drawing material suppliers).

b) Your map should be drawn on a suitable plastic drawing material, e.g. Imperial drafting film.

c) You will require a copy of the I.O.F. map symbols.

A large map takes a considerable amount of time (10 to 30 hours per square kilometre surveying for a full colour map) so do not be too ambitious. Try a small area first.

Contact your regional secretary. There may be an instructional course for mappers, which you may attend.

Glossary of Terms

Aiming-off	A method by which orienteers deliberately aim to one side of a control, especially a control placed on a linear feature.
Attack point	An easily identifiable point from which the final approach into control may be made.
Bearing	A method of indicating direction from one point to another, using the compass.
B.O.F.	British Orienteering Federation.
Contour interval	The vertical distance between contours. On 1:20,000 maps this is usually 25 feet (7.62 metres) but is increasingly 5.0m.
Control	A red and white marker banner, plus some means of recording one's visit to it (e.g. a punch).
Control description	A brief description of the feature on which a control is situated.
I.O.F.	International Orienteering Federation.
Leg	The distance from control to control.
Legend	The key or explanatory list of symbols used on the map.
Magnetic lines	Lines on an orienteering map pointing to Magnetic North.
Magnetic North	The direction to which the compass needle points.
Map correction	Additions or corrections to the map, usually posted near registration.
Map-memory	The skill of remembering the detail of the map.
Map scale	The relationship between a distance on the map and the corresponding horizontal distance on the ground.
Master map	The map on which the controls are marked and from which each competitor marks his or her own map at the start.
O.S.	Ordnance Survey.
Pace-counting	The measurement of distance using step counting (usually double steps).
Penetrability Index (Runnability or Feasibility)	A graduated scale of penetrability of vegetation, shown on a map by varying density of shading, usually green.
Pre-marked maps	Competitors' maps already printed with the controls.
Pre-start	The point where marshalling for the start occurs.
Registration	The point where the competitor initially reports, pays his fee, receives his map, etc.
"The Orienteer"	B.O.F. bi-monthly magazine.

Some Important Addresses

British Orienteering Federation,
National Office,
3 Glenfinlas Street,
Edinburgh, EH3 6YY.
B.O.F. Professional Officer:
  Tony Walker,
  7 Stocks Cottage,
  Wickens Corner,
  Beenham, Berkshire.
  Phone: Woolhampton 3427.
B.O.F. Honorary Secretary:
  Mrs. Susan Rogers,
  Linden Lodge,
  Lanchester, Co. Durham.
Regional Secretaries:
Scottish Orienteering Association:
  Mrs. E. Mills,
  92 Coillesdene Avenue,
  Edinburgh, EH15 2LG.
  Phone 031-669 1004
North Western Orienteering Association:
  Mrs. D. Griffiths,
  17 Rigby Lane, Bradshaw,
  Bolton, Lancashire.
  Phone Bolton 53869.
North Eastern Orienteering Association:
  Mrs. J. Brook,
  54 Valley Gardens,
  Whitley Bay, Northumberland.
           Phone Whitley Bay 23336.
Yorkshire and Humberside Orienteering Association:
  Brian Slater,
  102a Argyle Street, Hull HU3 1HG.
West Midlands Orienteering Association:
  Mike Griffin,
  Park Head Road, Dudley, Worcs.
East Midlands Orienteering Association:
  Ewen Cameron,
  60 Holywell Drive, Loughborough, Leics.
South West Orienteering Association:
  Mike Tween,
  88 Plantation Road, Poole, Dorset.
  Phone Broadstone 2063.
South Central Orienteering Association:
  David Bradnack,
  47 Thame Road, Haddenham, Bucks.
  Phone Haddenham 7269
South East Orienteering Association:
  Dr. David Thomas,
  16 Lambourne Drive,
  Bagshot, Surrey.
  Phone Bagshot 3298.
Welsh Orienteering Association:
  Mike Wilson,
  310 Fitzwilliam Wk., Castlefields,
  Runcorn, Cheshire.
Northern Ireland Orienteering Association:
  Graham Hamilton,
  Lilybank,
  Gilnakirk, Belfast 5.

East Anglian Orienteering Association
  Barry Sullivan,
  The Green, Wilby, Norwich.

Age Groups

Men

Older Veterans	50 years+
Veterans	43 years +
Senior Men	35 years +
Men	21 years +
Intermediates	19 - 20 years
Young men	17 - 18 years
Junior men	15 - 16 years
Boys	13 - 14 years
Young boys	12 and under

Women

Older Veterans	50 years+
Veterans	43 years +
Senior Women	35 years +
Women	19 years +
Young Women	17 - 18 years
Junior Women	15 - 16 years
Girls	13 - 14 years
Young girls	12 and under

References:

Orientierungslauf edited by Roman Bussman.

The Sport of Orienteering by Henderson and Kjellstrom

The Silva Compass Instructional Pamphlet.

Your Way With Map and Compass Orienteering by John Disley.

The Production of Orienteering Maps. B.O.F.

The Rules of Orienteering. B.O.F.

Orienteering by John Disley.

Acknowledgements

  S.O.A., St. Andrews University, D. Walkinshaw (Lenzie Academy).

  Heriot-Watt University Orienteering Club, Alloa Academy.

  Orienteering Club and Midland District of S.O.A. for the use of orienteering maps produced by them.

  Thanks to Mr. M. Booth, Dept. of P.E., McLaren High School, Callander, for his suggestions regarding the needs of the P.E. teacher introducing orienteering as a new school sport.

"PLAY THE GAME"

COACH YOURSELF ASSOCIATION FOOTBALL
by Allen Wade
F. A. Director of Coaching

Today is the day of the 'all round' footballer, the thinking player who is required to be a master of the game's full complement of skills. This new book, written by a man with a wealth of experience in training and coaching skills, is designed to cater for this new breed, and demonstrates the individual and tactical skills required by all competent footballers. The single volume is in four parts, dealing with these basic positions:

1. Goalkeeper
2. Back Defenders
3. Mid-Field Players
4. Strikers

The text is fully illustrated with explanatory diagrams and action photographs of world-famous players from an English First Division Football Club.

160 pages. *price* £1.00

THE TEACHING OF SWIMMING

This is a completely new edition of the Amateur Swimming Association's basic text book and incorporates the old 'Swimming Instruction.' It presents modern concepts of teaching swimming both to classes and individuals. It is an essential guide to all intending candidates for the Teachers Certificate Examination of the Association.

160 pages. Fully illustrated. *price* 55p

RIDING

Published at the request of the British Horse Society, this book is written to encourage young riders to appreciate the finer points of horsemanship. The contents include information about saddlery, grooming, care of the horse, common ailments, etc. Sketches show clearly the different rhythms of the horse in the walk, trot, canter and gallop, and the importance of complete co-ordination between rider and horse.

134 pages, over 120 illustrations. *price* 60p

CRICKET

The text and drawings of this book cover the basic techniques of all aspects of the game. The young cricketer can build up for himself a picture of how he should aim to play each stroke in batting, how he should try to bowl, whether he is fast, medium or spin bowler, and how he can improve his fielding, throwing and wicket-keeping. Produced for the M.C.C.

96 pages, over 100 illustrations. *price* 60p

LAWN TENNIS

Gives a detailed description of the principal strokes used in the game, showing the young player how to practise each stroke, how to use it, the cause and effect of mistakes in playing it.

144 pages, over 200 illustrations. *price* 60p

From your Bookshop or Sports Shop